Write for Results

Write for Results

Richard Lauchman

AMACOM NEW MEDIA
American Management Association
New York • Atlanta • Boston • Chicago • Kansas City • San Francisco • Washington, D. C.
Brussels • Mexico City • Tokyo • Toronto

This product is designed to provide accurate and authoritative information in regard to the subject matter covered. It is sold with the understanding that the publisher is not engaged in rendering legal, accounting, or other professional service. If legal advice or other expert assistance is required, the services of a competent professional person should be sought.

Library of Congress Cataloging-in-Publication Data

Lauchman, Richard.
    Write for results / Richard Lauchman.
    p. cm.
    Includes index.
    1. Business writing. I. Title.
HF5718.3.L383 1998
808'.06665—DC21   *97–52751*
                                   CIP

© 1998 AMACOM NEW MEDIA, a wholly owned subsidiary of American Management Association, New York.
All rights reserved.
Printed in the United States of America.

This product may not be reproduced,
stored in a retrieval system,
or transmitted in whole or in part,
in any form or by any means, electronic,
mechanical, photocopying, recording, or otherwise,
without the prior written permission of AMACOM NEW MEDIA,
a wholly owned subsidiary of American Management Association,
1601 Broadway, New York, NY 10019.

Printing number

10 9 8 7 6 5 4 3

Contents

Introduction	1
Part One: The Practical Writer	5
The Problem With "Style"	7
Toward a Definition of Style	9
Practical Thinking	13
1. A good writer works hard so that the reader won't have to.	13
2. The reader reads the words, not the mind.	14
3. The reader boils things down.	15
4. If you give the reader a chance to misunderstand you, he will take it.	15
5. The principal goal of good writing is to convey.	16
6. The meanings of words lie in the mind, not in the dictionary.	17
7. Good writing minimizes the chance of misunderstanding.	18
8. The complexity of the subject should be the only complexity in the writing.	19
9. In business, readers are ferociously impatient.	20
10. Good writing sounds like good speech.	22
11. Style must vary.	24

Part Two: Techniques for Conciseness and Emphasis — 27

On Being Concise — 29

What *Concise* Means — 29
What Conciseness Requires — 30

1. Write with verbs, not with nouns. — 31
2. State what the subject *does,* not what it is. — 32
3. Challenge adverbs. — 34
4. Don't worry about "passive" or "active"; just put the right word first and tell the truth. — 35
5. Find the word that captures the sense. — 38
6. Avoid redundancy. — 42
7. Avoid unnecessary repetition. — 52

On Being Emphatic — 54

8. Put words in subject-verb-object order. — 57
9. Place modifiers precisely. — 60
10. Hyphenate to create the appropriate emphasis. — 70
11. Keep equal ideas "parallel." — 75
12. Do not allow dogmatic folderol to interfere with plain style. — 80

On Choosing Words — 82

How to Find the Right Words — 85
Some Common Problems With Ordinary Words — 91

Part Three: Practical Punctuation — 103

Preliminary Remarks — 105
Precepts — 106

1. Punctuation cannot rescue sense from nonsense. — 106
2. Punctuation retards the reading. — 107
3. The reader reads what the writer writes. — 108
4. Punctuation is never "optional." — 109
5. Confusion often results when a mark plays different roles in a series. — 111
6. When you proofread someone else's writing, be conservative. — 111

Definitions — 112
The Marks — 115

Apostrophe (') — 115
Brackets [ ] — 119
Colon (:) — 120
Comma (,) — 123
Dash (—) — 130
Ellipsis points (. . .) — 132
Hyphen (-) — 133
Parentheses ( ) — 137
Period (.) — 139
Question Mark (?) — 140
Quotation Marks (" ") — 141
Semicolon (;) — 146
Slash (/) — 148

Relationships Between Clauses — 150

S V and V   One subject and two verbs. — 150
S and S V   Two subjects and one verb. — 150
IC IC   Two independent clauses without any conjunction. — 151
IC, and IC   Two independent clauses connected by a short conjunction. — 153

IC; however, IC Two independent clauses connected by a longer conjunction.	154
DC, IC A dependent clause followed by an independent clause.	155
IC DC An independent clause followed by a dependent clause.	156
IC, IC, and IC A list of three or more independent clauses.	156
IC [however, furthermore, therefore, etc.] IC	157
Punctuation at a Glance	158

Part Four: Electronic Writing 159

Electronic Mail 161

Electronic Mail at Home	162
Electronic Mail in the Workplace	163
Writing Effectively in Electronic Mail	165
1. Take extra care with the Subject line.	165
2. Come to the point.	166
3. Isolate a sentence to emphasize it.	169
4. Keep paragraphs short.	171
5. Check your spelling and punctuation.	171
6. Send it only to the right people.	174
7. Be courteous.	175
8. Keep it brief.	177
Some Warnings About Electronic Mail	177

Part Five: CD-ROM Functionality 181

Keyword Search	184
Select Specific Criteria	184
My Favorite Letters	186

Index 191

Write for Results

Introduction

Write for Results is the first title in the Get Ahead Toolkit series, which has been designed to help office professionals improve their skills and increase their value in the workplace—so they can get ahead in their careers.

The Get Ahead Toolkits offer the best of both worlds—the mobility and familiarity of a book combined with the interactivity of a CD-ROM. This combination creates a powerful learning tool. Research has shown that self-paced instruction is a much more effective way of learning and retaining information than traditional approaches.

Advantages of the Get Ahead Toolkits include:

- Interactivity—users decide what they want to learn and when to learn it (in the order that suits them best)
- Fun-to-use tools such as illustrations, bulleted checklists, quizzes, summaries, and valuable reference sections
- Well-designed interfaces that enable users to move through the program smoothly and efficiently—and always know where they are
- Expert sources since each CD-ROM and accompanying book is based on material from AMACOM, the publishing division of American Management Association International, the world leader in training businesspeople

Write for Results is an exciting learning program designed to help you improve your business writing skills by teaching you how to write powerful and efficient business documents. Effective business writing is a skill requiring knowledge and practice.

Write for Results offers supplementary reading on a number of useful topics such as:

- The problem with style
- Practical thinking
- On being concise
- On being emphatic
- On choosing words
- Punctuation
- Electronic writing

The CD-ROM is a practical tool that consists of a writing course, an on-line reference section, a library of boilerplate letters that can be easily adapted for your own personal use, and an evaluation section to test your knowledge.

In the Learn to Write for Results section you will be led through the process of constructing a clear, effective document. You will learn how to:

- Plan your document and its content
- Prepare your outline
- Write the first draft
- Check that it makes sense and will get the reaction you are seeking
- Ensure that it is readable and mechanically correct
- Use a suitable format for your document
- Edit and proofread it to eliminate errors

The Writer's Toolkit is a quick and easy-to-use reference section giving you additional information about grammar, spelling, punctuation, design, plain writing, and business writing etiquette. You will also find a useful list of common mistakes to avoid when writing.

In the Create Your Own Document section you will be able to try your hand at customizing over 300 standard letters, which have been taken from the business best-seller, *The AMA Handbook of Business Letters.* The letters cover many areas including sales, marketing, customer service, credit and collection, vendors and suppliers, personnel, confirmations, requests and responses, permission, cover letters—even social and personal correspondence.

Evaluate Your Writing Skills consists of four different tests, each containing twenty-five questions, which gives you the opportunity to test your knowledge of the English language and your ability to plan and write a draft document.

All these elements combine to make a thorough and entertaining way to learn new skills—in your own time and at your own pace.

Part One
The Practical Writer

The Problem With "Style"

> When I use a word, it means just what I choose it to mean—neither more nor less.
> —Humpty Dumpty, in *Through the Looking Glass*

Mr. Dumpty would find "style" to his liking. The word has been used so promiscuously that it now signifies nearly every aspect of writing—and when a person uses it, you can never be sure what he's talking about.

Style can mean whatever you want it to mean. Customer service departments give employees "style sheets" that suggest phrases to be used and phrases to be avoided (so certain phrases must be part of style). Most style sheets indicate the preferred format and typeface to be used as well (so format and typeface must be part of style). Corporations and government agencies distribute "style guides" that dictate the use of numbers, hyphens, capitalization, and just about any other aspect of standard usage you can imagine (so standard English must be part of style). *The Chicago Manual of Style* covers punctuation, grammar, and mechanics, so these must be part of style as well.

Style surely covers convention, too. The great majority of style guides feel an almost evangelical call to remind us, for example, not to split infinitives. A major telecommunications company's Proposal Preparation Guide puts the matter this way:

> A split infinitive occurs when an adverb appears between *to* and the infinitive it governs. NEVER USE SPLIT INFINITIVES!!!

Style can apply to spelling, as some authorities insist that *cancelling, travelling,* and *focussing* are "correct style," while others prefer *canceling, traveling,* and *focusing.* Some newspapers have dropped the letters *ue* from words like *demagogue, catalogue,* and *dialogue; The Washington Post* dropped the final *e* from *employee* (*employe* was their style of spelling) and then, in response to a surprising amount of mail, put it back on.

Style covers everything from abbreviations to symbols. Nothing is sacrosanct; no aspect of writing escapes. Style reaches out and lays its clammy fingers even on the number of a noun! A *Fortune* 100 company's Editorial Style Manual claims, for example, that "personnel" is *singular.* An example of its "correct" use—the example in the style guide—is this:

> All personnel is required to report to work by 8:30 A.M.

In my word processing software, style doesn't refer to any of these; it refers, instead, to my options of italicizing, underscoring, boldfacing, subscripting, or doing a number of other things to make the words stand out. So graphics must be part of style.

What *isn't* style? And how useful is a word that encompasses phrasing, format, typeface, punctuation, capitalization, abbreviations, the use of numbers, the use of hyphens, the meanings of words, the "correctness" of words, the spellings of words, whether you split an infinitive, whether you use personal pronouns, all of the above, none of the above, some of the above? When you say *style,* it means just what you choose it to mean—neither more nor less.

If style refers to everything, then it refers to nothing in particular. But in the practical world, where our goal is to communicate to others, words with loose definitions have no place; they reduce us to making noise when we're trying to make sense. And when a manager tells an employee, "Letters for my signature must be written in my style," we have an enigma parading as a sentence.

Toward a Definition of Style

If we are to discuss style in any meaningful way, we must first rescue the word from the wilderness of vague reference and assign it a precise meaning. A clear (and very useful) definition is possible, but it will make sense only if we agree on ten precepts.

First, let's agree that we are discussing business writing and nothing else. We are concerning ourselves with reports, proposals, memos, letters, and so forth: documents (1) that are written to make a point and (2) that the reader, in his day-to-day work, is obliged to read and understand. We are not concerning ourselves with documents that the reader chooses to read (novels, magazine articles, love letters, poems, and so forth), but only with the ones that he must read.

Second, let's agree that the nature of reading varies widely. We bring differing expectations to different kinds of documents: We expect a mystery story to keep us in suspense, but we expect the opposite from a memo. We tolerate and even enjoy ambiguity in a poem, but we expect clear language in a contract. In a letter from an old friend, we ignore errors in grammar and spelling—but do we ignore such errors when we read a sales letter or a proposal?

Third, let's agree that business documents receive a

"functional" reading. The expectations we bring to a business document differ from those we bring to any other kind of writing. We read not for entertainment but to discover what the writer wants us to do or to know. Therefore, we expect to encounter ideas, not to have to decipher stilted, awkward, or needlessly complex expressions—and certainly we expect to understand a sentence the first time we read it. In addition, we expect economy of expression: Business writing isn't poetry, and we do not treasure the writer's choice of words. If we encounter *notwithstanding the fact that*, we convert the sense to "although." Finally, we expect the document to make a point: Business writing isn't detective fiction, and if the point isn't in the first paragraph, we stop reading the sentences in order. We begin to scan.

Fourth, let's agree that there are rules and conventions governing the language, and that we will refer to the entire body of these rules and conventions as standard English. Those aspects of writing governed by standard English include grammar, punctuation, capitalization, the customary usage of words, and the spelling of words. We can agree that standard English is not fixed; we can agree that the language is in perpetual flux; we can agree that there are reasonable disputes about usage. What's important is that we accept this basic premise: There is a shared code that fosters communication, and the further one strays from that code, the less effective (clear, creditable, persuasive) one's writing becomes.

Fifth, let's agree that business writing must conform to standard English. Would anyone argue with this point? The purpose of business writing is to inform or to persuade, not to mystify. Business writing isn't experimental fiction, and writers who take liberties with standard spelling, grammar, and punctuation not only impose an undue burden on the reader but risk being judged as incompetent. In the competitive environment, credibility is a priceless commodity; when customers encounter sloppy writing, their reaction is swift and severe. You would certainly (and understandably) hesitate to award a contract to any company whose proposal was infested with errors in basic English. The subtextual message of sloppiness is inferred by all: The writer is negligent and inattentive (at best), or ignorant and unable (at worst). Such a response may not be noble, but it is quick and sure.

Sixth, let's agree that if sentences are (for any reason) incorrect, then style is not the issue. One who writes, "The problem with these proposals are that they are incomplete" is guilty not of poor style but of poor grammar. One who writes, "The policy will enable us to accomodate the needs of all employees" is guilty not of poor style but of poor spelling. In a sentence such as "Our Senior auditor Donald Marks, visited the Banks headquarters on May 18," the issue is not style; punctuation and capitalization are simply incorrect.

Seventh, let's agree that so long as people conform to standard English, they are entitled to write in any way they prefer. Let's see where this liberalism gets us. Joe can write, "The advertising campaign must be simplified." Stansfield is free to write, "The product recognition program is in need of a substantial amelioration enhancement." Both sentences conform to the conventions of standard English; both are, in an abstract universe, identical in terms of "perfection."

Eighth, let's agree that in the practical world both the writer and his readers pay a price for needless complexity. While Stansfield's style is perfectly legitimate, it is a style best reserved for his Great American Novel, his diary, his poetry, or his mumbling to himself. In the world of work, the result of Stansfield's "style" is (1) Stansfield's risking a reputation as a bully and (2) communication ruptured, trust lost, time wasted, money squandered.

Ninth, let's agree that we would rather read Joe's sentence than Stansfield's sentence. Anyone who would rather read Stansfield's sentence is excused from writing in the business environment and should go to Paris, wear a black beret, frequent bistros, and revel in syllables. Joe's sentence is simple and embodies everything that is good about writing: It is effortless reading.

Tenth, let's agree that the Golden Rule is a good one to apply to writing and that if we prefer to read Joe's sentence, then we should write Joe's sentence. Here we see the first glimmers of what style truly is; because anyone who could write a sentence like Stansfield's could—merely that, merely *could*—write a sentence like Joe's.

"Style takes its final shape more from attitudes of mind than from principles of composition," Mr. Strunk wrote succinctly in *The Elements of Style*. This is the heart of the matter: Anyone who writes like Stansfield chooses to do so.

Since Stansfield could, if he'd wanted to, have written Joe's sentence, his skill with language isn't the issue. His judgment is the issue. If business writing is to improve, we must understand that style is best understood to be the by-product of the writer's judgment. Stansfield's style manifests his judgment; his judgment, in turn, is based on his attitudes (about words, about himself, about the occasion, and toward his reader) and on his assumptions about the interaction called reading. If we can agree that, in business writing, any style that interferes with readability is a bad style, then Stansfield's style is a poor one. But it is also easily improved. All that is required of Stansfield is that he (1) practice good faith in writing and (2) adopt more practical assumptions about what his readers need.

We'll turn now to what Mr. Strunk called attitudes of mind: those assumptions that form the soil of judgment.

Practical Thinking

To write in plain style, we need to think about writing in a certain way (a way that might be called practical). Our assumptions about writing—what it should look and sound like, what it should accomplish, and so forth—not only manifest themselves in every sentence we write, but they dictate style. The quitch seed will produce quitch (a weed); the acorn gives rise to the oak. Planted in mud, they both die. And if our assumptions about writing are off the mark, then our skill with language is meaningless. We will write complex and impractical stuff.

Certain assumptions complicate style; others foster simplicity. Here are the ones that foster simplicity. Make them your own.

1. A good writer works hard so that the reader won't have to.

Writing is easy. Writing well requires effort. A document that is easy to write will usually be imprecise and difficult to understand. It is easy, for example, for the writer to toss out *Modifications to the text are needed in order for there to be a lessened opportunity for miscomprehension.* It requires more effort to pick precise words and engineer them into the right order: *To minimize the chance of misunderstanding, we must clarify the policy.* Make things easy for the reader.

In brutally practical terms, if a writer spends fifteen minutes on a document, but a dozen readers must spend ten minutes each deciphering it (and calling the writer to ask her what she meant), then the communication costs 135 minutes. If the writer spends thirty minutes on the document, simplifying it so that the dozen readers need to spend only two minutes each, then the communication costs only fifty-four minutes. This very conservative example should suggest an important point: In a world where time and money equate, the responsible writer takes the time to be clear.

2. The reader reads the words, not the mind.

Your reader isn't clairvoyant; he cannot read your mind. His only responsibility is to read what you actually write. He should never need to guess at a meaning; he should never encounter ambiguity and be forced to interpret an expression. In the sentence below, how is the estate to be divided?

> Mr. O'Connell stipulated that his estate be equally divided among his wife, his brother Kevin, and Michael and Sean, his sons.

Michael and Sean understand the sentence to mean that the estate is to be divided four ways; Mrs. O'Connell and Kevin understand it to mean that the estate is to be divided three ways. Each "interpretation" has merit. Litigation will certainly ensue, and attorneys will enjoy a handsome profit because of this poorly organized and unclear sentence.

The reader is at the writer's mercy, and when she reads, *The falling dollar will radically affect American exports*, she is forced to guess at the meaning. The writer knows that the decreased value of the dollar will *stimulate* exports, or *decrease* exports, but if he does not use those words, then the reader does not read them. The writer's knowing what he means is important—but his job is to let the reader in on the secret.

3. The reader boils things down.

When reading business documents, we reduce every expression to its simplest and essential meaning. When we encounter *in the vicinity of*, we extract the sense of "near"; when we encounter *in consideration of the fact that*, we glean the sense of "because." And we are neither fooled nor impressed by *prior to*—we dig around in those words and unearth the sense of "before." The writer should provide the simple word.

Business writing should be effortless reading. The reader of business documents should not be forced to extract, glean, or dig around in phrases like a woebegone archaeologist. Writers who believe that *at this point in time* is a professional way to say *now* are forgetting that readers refine the sense of *now* from that complex phrase. The practical writer does not make the reader work. Be concise.

4. If you give the reader a chance to misunderstand you, he will take it.

Readers are notoriously perverse this way. Presented with the least ambiguity, they will snatch a meaning other than the one the writer intended. What is the meaning of the following, innocent-looking expression?

> All of these ideas are not relevant.

The writer wants to convey that some of the ideas are irrelevant—but the reader understands that *all* of the ideas are irrelevant. Can we blame her? The second meaning haunts the expression just as surely as the first. And is the reader responsible for misinterpreting the idea? According to Assumption 2, the reader should never be faced with the need to interpret. The writer is always responsible for ambiguity. No reader should need to make sense of an idea. Making sense is the writer's job.

5. The principal goal of good writing is to convey.

Clarity alone is not the goal, because an expression can be clear and yet convey a sense other than the one the writer intended. And while vague writing provokes calls for clarification, clear writing does not. Clear writing will be accepted on its face.

> The annual USOG membership fee is $5, which includes a spouse at no extra charge.

That sentence unequivocally promises a spouse for a $5 fee. That is not what the writer means, of course. It is merely what she writes. "Oh," she says with a little wave of the hand, "readers know what I mean." The argument that readers use common sense is a reasonable one. They do. The counter-arguments are more to the point: (1) Should the reader be forced into a "detective" mode? (2) Is the reader the only one who can use common sense? (3) Does the credibility of the writer count at all? (4) What are the limits of interpretation? (5) Is such writing good enough?

Business writing abounds with entertaining sentences like the ones that follow, all of which are dizzyingly "clear."

> The tornado in my opinion is an Act of God.
> You can't count the trees still standing on your fingers.
> The employee claims that rude comments were made by the water cooler on the eighth floor.
> We're confident that once you try a pair of our jeans, you'll never want to wear another.

All convey clear ideas, but none convey what the writer intended. Most readers can figure out what the writer meant to say—which is the writer's job—but what of the writer's credibility? The dull yellow gleam of inattention (or worse) glimmers in such sentences, and readers are right to look askance at the source.

6. The meanings of words lie in the mind, not in the dictionary.

At first glance, this idea may seem anarchic; on reflection, it may seem simplistic. But it is a law as unyielding as gravity, and writers forget it at their peril. Practically speaking, the purpose of business writing is to inform or persuade—not to enthrall, impress, or improve the vocabulary of the reader, and certainly not to hazard misunderstanding. Good writers are aware of the mischief lurking in the following sentence.

> Beginning January 1, cost analyses must be filed bimonthly, rather than monthly.

The fun begins here. The writer, believing that *bimonthly* means "every two months," presumes he had made his meaning clear. The reader, believing that *bimonthly* means "twice per month," assumes she understands the idea. Because she thinks she knows the word's meaning, she does not look it up in the dictionary.

On January 15 or 16, cost analyses begin to arrive on the surprised writer's desk. Now the fun gets going in earnest. The parties scurry to the dictionary, eager to ascertain what the word truly "means." Both meanings are there. The writer is gratified to see that the first meaning is "every two months"; the reader is relieved to see that "twice per month" follows on its heels.

And now the party is in full swing. "Look here," the writer says. "The first definition is *every two months*." The reader rounds on him. "And it also means what I thought it meant. Twice a month. It's in the dictionary!"

Knowing what the dictionary says is handy, but knowing how the reader understands a word is essential. Simple words minimize the chance that a reader will misconstrue the meaning; here, since the writer meant "every two months," the phrase *every two months* would have been simple and immediately clear.

7. Good writing minimizes the chance of misunderstanding.

To maximize the clarity of your writing, use the words you learned first. That's what "keep it simple" means. Rather than *prioritize desirable outcomes*, a good writer will rank goals; rather than *elucidate the protocol*, a good writer will clarify the policy. Don't erect a cathedral when a pup tent will suffice.

Unseasoned writers, especially those fresh from college and graduate school, often sleepwalk under the spell of big words. They fly to Latinate language the way iron shavings fly to a magnet; they will write *orientate* when they mean "point" and *terminate* when they mean "stop." They do so from the misconception that *utilize, bifurcate, definitize,* and *delineate* are somehow more professional than *use, divide, define,* and *outline*. The big Latinate words aren't more professional; in fact, because they require more time and guesswork from the reader, they are less so.

Subsequent to receiving your memo, I canceled the contract.

The Problem With "Style"

If the writer is confident that all of his readers understand *subsequent to* to mean "after," then *subsequent to* will convey his meaning. If, however, one reader out of one hundred—for any reason, ranging from ignorance to haste—understands the phrase to mean "before," then the writer has chosen poorly. (He might be surprised to learn that five out of ten adult Americans either don't know what *subsequent to* means or confuse it with *before*.) He can insist until the very last cow comes home that *subsequent to* means "after"; he can shake a dictionary in the reader's face, point to the small print, and sputter something about a definition. His being correct on the point changes nothing: At the crucial moment, the reader has misunderstood him.

The argument that adults should know the meaning of *subsequent to* is more than elitist—it is irrelevant and vain. Work with the words you are certain your readers do know. Ultimately and inarguably, *after* is the right word if the writer means "after." It is the right word because it minimizes—not abrogates or obviates—the chance of misunderstanding. The good writer never has to resort to a dictionary to prove himself "right." The mere fact of his needing to do that proves he used bad judgment.

8. The complexity of the subject should be the only complexity in the writing.

In the complicated world of business and technical writing, where shrapnel flies disguised as *kinetic energy chunky fragments* and a research paper is formally designated a *unimolecular chemical degradation reaction study*, does it make sense to complicate further? The writer may be obliged to use a squirming noun—but no one picks his verb for him, and he alone selects his adjective. Is clarity improved when he chooses *went into sudden incendiary mode* over *ignited* or *infundibuliform* over *funnel-shaped*?

Needless complexity is the hallmark of a bad writer. When the big words slither into the sentence, simplicity takes wing. In writing, simplicity is the chief good; when writing is simple, it is easy to understand. It will not be simplistic unless the writer has failed to think things through. *Simplistic* describes oversimplified thought, not the expression of thought. When one ignores the complexity inherent in an event, fails to anticipate and answer the reader's questions, or disregards the reader's probable objections, then the thinking is simplistic. No degree of simplicity will rescue simplistic thought; no degree of needless complexity will long disguise it.

Do not complicate. This animal is not a *feline*, but a cat; this cat does not *masticate*, but chews; it does not chew its *sustenance*, but its food. Anyone who sees a cat chewing its food and actually thinks, "There is a sustenance-masticating feline" should be excused from writing in business; there is no hope for him.

9. In business, readers are ferociously impatient.

Their impatience is practical and stems from a series of expectations about business writing. The writer must understand and accept these expectations so that she can work to fulfill them.

When we read something for pleasure (a novel, feature article, or letter from an old friend), we expect a storytelling sort of presentation, a rambling journey through ideas. We demand to be kept in suspense by a good mystery story; we don't care whether our friend's letter contains a bottom-line point. But we read such documents because we choose to read them. Because we choose to read them, we disregard wordiness, lack of focus, personal quirks of style, and even errors in standard usage. The reading is relaxed and temperate.

Business documents are read with a completely different set of expectations. In business, documents receive a *functional* reading, and for this reason they must be written functionally. Keep the following ideas firmly in mind:

• *Readers expect you to come to the point.* Readers expect business documents to make a particular point, and they are vexed when the point is buried or (worse) never actually stated anywhere in the text. Readers of business documents expect the bottom line to be revealed in the first paragraph; if it isn't, they will certainly not behave as readers of love letters do (plucking and tasting every plum of a word and reading all the sentences in order), but they will ransack the text, rummaging impatiently until they find the point. If you begin with background or inexplicable detail, readers will skip it. They will skim until they discover what you want them to do or to know. Since this is how people read, it makes good sense to put your important ideas in the first paragraph, if not in the first sentence. Readers who hunger for background, explanation, or justification can keep reading; those uninterested in such details can stop.

• *Readers expect economy of expression.* Descriptive writing is appropriate in a novel; wordiness is overlooked in personal letters. But the language of business documents should be as concise as you can make it. The reader is justifiably impatient with *on two separate and distinct occasions*, when all the writer means is "twice"; the reader is right to snort with exasperation when he must hack his way through *performed a thorough and complete investigation of*. He could have leapt nimbly over *thoroughly investigated*.

• *Readers expect you to use words they understand.* If you're reading an article for pleasure and encounter the word *quondam,* you are free either to guess at its meaning or to look it up in the dictionary. Your knowing what it means isn't crucial; you don't need to do anything or decide anything, your reputation is not at risk, and money will not change hands. But if you encounter that word in a business document, you have no choice but to interrupt the reading and grab the dictionary (in business, guessing can be very expensive). Readers of business documents should never be obliged to look a word up! *Nunc pro tunc* may seem like a ripsnorting way to say *retroactively,* but a *nunc pro tunc* on a page to be read by anyone other than attorneys and scholars is the footprint of a bonehead. And it is chronic boneheadedness to insist that difficult words and phrases are appropriate merely because they happen to exist in some dictionary. The purpose of a memo is to convey something, not to mystify or impress. The bonehead writes *apposite* to prove he was there; the good writer writes *appropriate* and leaves no trace of himself.

• *Readers expect you to conform to standard English.* When people notice errors in the writing, they stop reading and begin to edit. A reader who encounters a misspelled word, a word used in the wrong way (such as *imply* when the sense is *infer*), a semicolon when a comma is required, or any other elementary error will cease seeing your ideas and begin scrutinizing the mechanics of language. This is not what reading should be. Let no quirk, flourish, error, or awkwardness distract from the ideas themselves. In business writing, good style is the absence of "style."

10. Good writing sounds like good speech.

"Good" speech is the key. Good speech communicates, with a minimum of fuss and bother, what the speaker intends;

The Problem With "Style" 23

thus, a reasonable person keeps her speech simple. Only someone recently released from the asylum of business school would actually say,

> Our new advertising campaign will systematize positive corporate product image consolidation in the potential targeted customer base.

Mercifully, very few people actually hear such words come out when they open their mouths. Very few people think in such a monstrous manner. Why, then, do we read such writing? We read it because people believe that writing must differ from speech. They are right about that, but they are wrong about the nature of the difference: Writing should not be more "elevated" or "elegant" than good speech. It should simply be more precise.

But let's not leap from an airy height into muck. The oft-given instruction "Write the way you speak" is hardly the panacea. Taken on face value (which is how most people take things), "Write the way you speak" invites chaos. Unlike the listener, the reader has no access to the inflections of the voice; unless the writer puts words in the right order and punctuates appropriately, nuance and emphasis are lost. Unlike the speaker, the writer isn't present at the moment of communication and cannot react to an eyebrow raised in confusion. Writers must be far more deliberate than speakers. Furthermore, speaking is a much more relaxed activity than writing is, and most speakers, even highly educated ones, are often imprecise. A reasonable person might say, for example,

> In light of the fact that we only heard about the incident yesterday, we'll need more time to do an investigation.

Grammar here is fine, and the thought is fairly clear. The sentence suffers from the minor problems of wordiness and loose emphasis. If someone spoke that sentence, the listener would hear how *only* modifies *yesterday*, but the reader doesn't hear the writer's inflection. For this reason, writers should put words in precise order. Note, in the revision below, that the writer uses the same conversational English words; he merely places them exactly where they should go and simplifies wherever he can.

> Because we heard about the incident only yesterday, we need more time to investigate.

11. Style must vary.

Don't confuse "style" with "professional tradition." There are good reasons why scientific reports need to be dispassionate and objective, good reasons why contracts and other legal documents need to be impersonal, good reasons why proposals need to contain technical terms. In a scientific report, *It was demonstrated that gravity excludes extraneous electrons* is a perfectly fine sentence if what did the demonstrating is either obvious or irrelevant. In a legal brief, tradition justifies such sentences as *Plaintiff contends, pursuant to 24 U.S. 311, that said affidavit is invalid.* In a technical proposal, *The AVM enables the COTA to oscillate at 600 rps* is appropriate, so long as the intended reader is familiar with the abbreviations.

What's important to understand is that readers of scientific documents expect an "objective" approach, judges expect legal "terms of art," and contracting officers expect technical detail. In every profession, traditions evolve—traditions regarding point of view, word choice, format, and so on—and these traditions establish the accepted idiom (or stylistic preferences) of a profession. When writing to members of a particular profession, writers are free to use the idiom of that profession. Since the tradition is what readers expect, arbitrarily deviating from it can backfire—not only can the deviation distract, but it can also provoke readers to wonder about the writer's expertise (and thus his credibility).

But there is a difference between conforming to a tradition simply because it is a tradition and conforming to it because it is a sensible and useful one. We must wonder whether the judge who expects *the aforesaid appeal herein* truly prefers to read such language or whether he feels doomed to read it. My guess is the latter. My guess is that readers of scientific documents feel obliged—fated—to slog through *current genetic reconfiguration methodologies*, and would tell you, if you asked them and they were honest, that they would rather read about *current methods for modifying genes*.

The jargon of law, the compact syntax of science, the abbreviations of engineers—while these may contribute to precision after two or three readings, they are difficult enough for the readers who expect them. (We can call these readers sacred, because they belong to a particular priesthood.) Clearly, when these idiomatic traditions escape their professions and encounter secular readers (i.e., those uninitiated in the mysteries), communication abruptly stops. When a customer inquires about a problem with her telephone service, such a response as *The outdial blockage consequented from a digital switching relay malfunction in the trunkline at T2* may as well be the yodelings of a Siberian husky.

Adjust your style to accommodate the reader and the occasion. Precision does not matter if it is expressed in a language foreign to the reader, and a memo thanking paralegals for contributing to a charity does not need to be written in the formidable lingo of a Memorandum Opinion and Order. The *It was thought that* and *It was observed that* of science have no place in a letter to a customer, and mysterious remarks like *EATU* (European/Asian Trafficking Unit) and *TDMA* (Time-Deferred Multiple Access) must be confined within the temple walls. Use sacred language when you converse with priests, but when you have a secular or general audience, relax the formal idiom of your profession. A man wearing a tuxedo while tossing a Frisbee to his dog might make an interesting spectacle in a television commercial, but in the practical world that person would be carefully watched.

PART TWO
Techniques for Conciseness and Emphasis

On Being Concise

What *Concise* Means

Of all the myths about writing, the one that provokes the most mischief is that *Be concise* means "Be brief." Conciseness and brevity are hardly the same thing, and writers who confuse the two create cryptic, impenetrable, or ambiguous expressions.

> We need to modernize our obsolete nuclear weapons tracking system.

We're guessing if we think we know what's obsolete in that simple sentence. No hyphen alerts us to whether certain words form a unit; *obsolete* could relate to *weapons* or to *system*. If we read by the code of ordinary syntax, we'd assume that the writer means:

> We need to modernize our obsolete system for tracking nuclear weapons.

Unfortunately, the writer intends to convey something quite different:

> We need to modernize our system that tracks obsolete nuclear weapons.

The clear expression of the thought requires six words, not five. If an expression isn't clear on the first reading, then the fact that it's presented in five words (as opposed to six) is beside the point. If six or seven or a dozen words are required to convey an idea, then that is the number of words the writer should use. Conciseness demands not that we minimize the number of words in a sentence, but that we make every word count.

What Conciseness Requires

At its heart, being concise requires that writers (1) know the meanings of words, (2) choose precise words, (3) let definitions do the job, (4) remember what the reader already knows, and (5) be willing to tell the plain truth. All wordiness proceeds from the writer's disregarding one or more of these issues.

If we know the meaning of *postpone*, we would never write *put off until a later time*; if we know the meaning of *twice*, we would not write *on two separate and distinct occasions*. If we choose precisely, we write that an event *jeopardizes* a project, not that the event *negatively affects the potential success of* the project; we would write that a remark *bewildered* an audience, not that it *had the effect of leaving the audience in a very confused state*. If we respect definitions, we write of our experience and of the forecast, not of our *past experience* and of the *forecast for the future*. If the reader already knows, because the writer has already said so, that a report presents the results of the Consumer Confidence Poll of July 1993, then repeating *the July 1993 Consumer Confidence Poll report* is wordiness in the extreme. The word *report* would suffice.

Finally, if the writer has something to say, she should say it. If the truth of the matter is "Because of the cost overruns, I decided to cancel the contract," then *Due to the ongoing nature of the contractor's billings exceeding the terms provided in the contract, the decision to terminate the contract was made* is worse than merely wordy. It borders on deception.

Good faith. Two little words, but how important. With good faith, you need only practice technique, and conciseness will follow. Without good faith—here, *the attempt to communicate honestly*—no degree of technical skill with language will make the slightest difference.

Here are techniques that will make your writing concise. Examples are given to illustrate the techniques; in general, the examples in the column on the left are wordy and inexact, while the revisions on the right are succinct and precise.

1. Write with verbs, not with nouns.

If you write, *The species is making a return to populated areas*, you are using *return* as a noun. Use it as a verb instead, and your writing will be much more concise: *The species is returning to populated areas*. If you write, *We gave them warning that they would have a need to create an increase in their capital reserves*, you are using *warning*, *need*, and *increase* as nouns, and the sentence is imprecise. Used as verbs, these words force precision: *We warned them that they would need to increase their capital reserves*.

Write with verbs, not with nouns. Following this instruction will make your writing clearer, more succinct, and more emphatic. When you look for a verb, ask yourself, "What, precisely, does the subject do?" Observe the patterns in the examples below, and notice how the exact verb simplifies and invigorates the expression.

They will perform an audit of the bank next week.	They will audit the bank next week.
He made the attempt to create documentation of the problem.	He tried to document the problem.
They have made the promise to provide funding for the venture.	They have promised to fund the venture.
When we made a visit to the site, we took a tour of the missile complex.	When we visited the site, we toured the missile complex.
They performed an appraisal of the property after they did a survey of the lot.	They appraised the property after they surveyed the lot.
Our competitors are putting their reputation in jeopardy by not putting as much emphasis as they used to on customer service.	Our competitors are risking their reputation by deemphasizing customer service.
She did an analysis of the demographics and makes the claim that there will be shrinkage in our customer base.	She analyzed the demographics and claims that our customer base will shrink.
The CEO gave a speech about the importance of manifesting ethical behavior.	The CEO spoke about the importance of behaving ethically.
Readers show a preference for simplicity and do a skimming of difficult material.	Readers prefer simplicity and skim difficult material.
He gave the report that the client was exhibiting an interest in the device.	He reported that the client was interested in the device.
They did a monitoring of the site and made the discovery that the species was making a rapid recovery.	They monitored the site and discovered that the species was rapidly recovering.

2. State what the subject *does*, not what it is.

Your writing will become more concise if you minimize your use of the *to be* verb (*is, am, are, be, being, been, was, were*).

On Being Concise

Instead of telling the reader what the subject is, always try to express precisely what the subject *does*. Note how emphasis improves in the following examples.

The surgeon is in vigorous opposition to the procedure.	The surgeon vigorously opposes the procedure.
The attorney's remark was very confusing to the witness.	The attorney's remark perplexed the witness.
They are still of the firm belief that the advertising is misleading to consumers.	They remain convinced that the advertising misleads consumers.
He is adamant that he was under the impression that the test was in compliance with FDA regulations.	He insists that he thought the test complied with FDA regulations.
She is the chairperson of the committee that is in oversight of the funding.	She chairs the committee that oversees funding.
This response is typical of their attitude about deadlines.	This response typifies their attitude about deadlines.
He was successful in his attempt to be persuasive to the vice president regarding the funding of the program.	He succeeded in persuading the vice president to fund the program.
Ms. Fox will be the representative of our organization at the conference.	Ms. Fox will represent us at the conference.

Use good judgment. Certainly you will sometimes need to use an *is* (and its cousins). Whenever the emphasis of the expression requires a form of the *to be* verb, use it in good faith.

> Complying with regulations *is impossible* when the regulations *are ambiguous*.
> Since the situation *is unprecedented*, we *are unsure* how to respond.

In those sentences, *is* and *are* indicate states of being; they do their job perfectly well, and it makes no sense to spend time considering how one might revise them.

3. Challenge adverbs.

Adverbs are often unnecessary and should always be challenged. If you write *proceeded very slowly*, challenge the *very slowly*. Would "crept" convey the idea more precisely? When you write *look closely at*, chances are good that you mean "scrutinize"; if you write *decline precipitously*, you probably mean "plunge."

Find the one-word verb that captures your meaning. Note the precision, vigor, and emphasis that this technique creates in the examples on the right.

The shareholders responded negatively to the proposal.	The shareholders rejected the proposal.
The shareholders reacted enthusiastically to the decision.	The shareholders applauded the decision.
The board of directors thought carefully about the merger.	The board of directors deliberated the merger.
The consultant spoke indistinctly as he went quickly through the material.	The consultant mumbled as he hurried through the material.
The reasons for the decline will be clearly presented in the report.	The reasons for the decline will be stated in the report.
Economists claim that the GNP is growing negatively at a 2 percent rate.	Economists claim that the GNP is shrinking at a 2 percent rate.
Economists' statements are often nearly impossible to understand.	Economists' statements frequently defy comprehension.

On Being Concise

After she looked quickly at the report, she walked angrily from the office.	After she glanced at the report, she stormed from the office.
The consensus quickly fell apart when the news came.	The consensus collapsed when the news came.
Our employees' morale is slowly being eaten away by the litigation.	Our employees' morale is being eroded by the litigation.
This report indicates that the infrastructure is slowly losing its integrity.	This report indicates that the infrastructure is disintegrating.

4. Don't worry about "passive" or "active"; just put the right word first and tell the truth.

Many people blame the passive voice for most of the ills in business writing. To do so is to generalize in the worst way. The passive is frequently necessary, and writers who believe it is "bad" or "weak" will often emphasize the wrong idea.

Let's make very certain that we understand what we're talking about. A sentence is said to be active when the subject acts; it is said to be passive when the subject receives the action.

Active	Passive
The Redskins beat the Eagles.	The Eagles were beaten by the Redskins.
We received the imagery analysis today.	The imagery analysis was received today.

If we ask which of those are better sentences, we have asked a meaningless question. All are fine. All are simple, emphatic, and free of clutter. The active sentences emphasize the Redskins and the *we*; the passive sentences emphasize the Eagles and the imagery analysis. The question with teeth is this:

What do you intend to emphasize? What are you going to talk about in the sentences that follow? Emphasis should determine which word you use as the subject of the sentence. Once you've decided what to emphasize, all you need to do is tell the truth. The following sentences are perfectly reasonable.

The issue was not decided by the committee.	*Passive; emphasizes* issue, *and the writer will go on to discuss the issue.*
The committee adjourned before deciding the issue.	*Active; emphasizes* committee, *and the writer will go on to discuss the committee.*
Writers should use the passive voice in good faith.	*Active; emphasizes* writers, *and the writer will go on to discuss writers.*
The passive voice should be used in good faith.	*Passive; emphasizes* the passive voice, *and the writer will go on to discuss the passive voice.*

Few adults actually write such awkward-sounding sentences as *Your remarks are appreciated by me* or *The report was written by me.* When you see an expression like that, the fault lies not with the passive construction but with the assumption that has produced the construction: Somewhere along the line, the writer was told very forcefully that he must never, ever use *I* in formal writing.

The sentences below are passive and are perfectly clear.

We were flabbergasted by the results.	*Stresses how we were affected.*
The audit will be completed next week.	*Stresses the audit, not the auditors.*
These questions are ambiguously phrased.	*Who wrote the questions is irrelevant.*
The mistakes have been corrected.	*Who corrected the mistakes is irrelevant.*
Their objection was unexpected.	*Who failed to expect it is obvious.*

On Being Concise

The passive voice can contribute to poor writing, but blaming it for sentences such as the ones below is like blaming the airwaves for nonsense on television. The fault lies with the originating mind, which gets the logic backwards.

Reading this document is forbidden by those persons without "top-secret" clearance.	*Persons without "top-secret" clearance are doing the forbidding?*
The handling of laboratory animals is strictly prohibited by unauthorized personnel.	*The unauthorized personnel are prohibiting others?*
Legislation is being considered to reduce the COLA in the House of Representatives.	*The House is considering reducing its own cost-of-living adjustment?*

The following sentences in the left column may be passive, but wild syntax and big words are what interfere with clarity. Converting them to the active voice helps, but simpler words help more.

It was demonstrated that the effect of elevated temperature on the compound was negligible by this experiment.	This experiment demonstrated that increased heat has little effect on the compound.
That she was accosted by the D section lamppost in the parking lot is alleged and maintained by the complainant.	The complainant states that she was accosted near the D section lamppost in the parking lot.
There were no apparent reasons why the determination was made by EPA of endangered species classification in the report.	The report failed to indicate why EPA has classified the species as "endangered."

The sentence in the left column below is passive, but the main difficulty with it is its length. A good writer never makes a reader work so hard.

The failure to report the overrun within the time specified by the contract and according to procedures therein was attributed to a new project manager's being uncertain about the requirements by OSI.	According to OSI, the overrun was not reported promptly because the new project manager was unaware of the requirement to do so.

Don't despise the passive voice. Use it when emphasis and context demand its use. It is senseless to try to make every sentence active; when you do that, you alter emphasis.

Active: The Redskins beat the Eagles. [*Credits the Redskins.*]
Passive: The Eagles were beaten by the Redskins. [*Emphasizes the Eagles but credits the Redskins.*]
Active: The Eagles lost to the Redskins. [*Does not credit the Redskins.*]

5. Find the word that captures the sense.

Some people believe that a lengthy expression better emphasizes an idea than a brief expression does. Paradoxically, the opposite is true: *Fire!* bursts into the mind far more readily than does *For reasons of an incipient incendiary event, it is strongly recommended that immediate evacuation of the premises be undertaken.*

Length dilutes; brevity emphasizes. Needless words dilute emphasis in precisely the same way that too much water weakens tea.

A halt to the ongoing exceeding of the contract by the costs associated with the program is absolutely imperative.	The overruns must stop.
In close proximity to Mount St. Helens, seismic tremors have begun to occur at thirty-second intervals of time.	Near Mount St. Helens, tremors now occur every thirty seconds.

On Being Concise

Our experience in the past gives the strong indication that adding additional incentives seldom if ever has the result of convincing customers to purchase automotive units.	Our experience strongly indicates that added incentives seldom induce customers to buy cars.

When the writer finds the right word, she doesn't need a lot of almost-right ones to make her point. When we write *from time to time* or *once in a while*, we mean "occasionally"; when we write *as a general rule*, we mean "usually" or "generally." Don't define the word in the sentence.

The police are now of the suspicion that the fire was intentionally set.	The police now suspect arson.
His argument went here and there and all over the place, apparently without a goal.	His argument wandered aimlessly.
It is our conclusion that a spark caused the boxes to burst into flame.	We conclude that a spark ignited the boxes.
She embodies an example of a good manager.	She exemplifies good management.
The clause contains several plausible interpretations.	The clause is ambiguous.
Employees must on an interim basis use the lounge on the third floor.	Employees must temporarily use the lounge on the third floor.

Think with individual words, not with phrases. Fitting the flesh of words onto the spirit of ideas is an activity as mysterious as conjuring, and each of us is a sorcerer. But what would we think of a sorcerer who tried to conjure a hummingbird and called up a hippo instead? We would see a fat walloping hippo, and the sorcerer's insistence that he *meant* a hummingbird would not change what we see. Avoid the packaged phrases. The lumbering expressions below all mean "because":

> in light of the fact that
> in view of the fact that
> in consideration of the fact that
> because of the fact that
> due to the fact that
> given the fact that
> for the reason that
> inasmuch as
> on account of
> on the grounds that
> owing to the fact that

Indiscriminately spewing the first words that come to mind is a good idea when you are drafting the document. When you revise, discriminate: Replace the spewed phrase with a precise word. Notice the improvement in the sentences on the right.

Owing to the fact that Colonel Senchak has diplomatic immunity, conducting a prosecution of him is well outside the realm of possibility.	Because Colonel Senchak has diplomatic immunity, prosecuting him is impossible.
Dr. Wells was interrupted only on one distinct occasion, but the interruption lasted for a thirty-minute period of time.	Dr. Wells was interrupted only once, but the interruption lasted thirty minutes.
She has on numerous occasions made the attempt to provide reasons for her decision.	She has often tried to explain her decision.

On Being Concise

We are making the request that you provide payment in a timely manner.	We ask that you pay promptly.
We tried on two separate occasions to bring the variables to a minimum.	We tried twice to minimize the variables.
We are at this point in time of the opinion that gravity waves are the reason for the disturbance.	We currently believe that gravity waves cause the disturbance.
In the final analysis, good writing is a reflection of an honest mind.	Ultimately, good writing reflects honesty.
Beginning this year and continuing indefinitely into the future, distribution of dividends will be made on an annual basis.	From now on, dividends will be paid annually.
Despite the fact that he is, as a general rule, hard to pin down precisely, Senator Karp on this occasion gave a complete, precise, and thorough response to the question that was put to him.	Although he is usually evasive, Senator Karp answered the question thoroughly and precisely.
The vice president made the request that we abbreviate the presentation to make it less time-consuming.	The vice president asked us to shorten the presentation.
The software costs the sum of $4,000, but due to the fact that it will make it simpler for us to keep track of indirect costs, it is my opinion that the purchase of it is practical.	The software costs $4,000, but because it will simplify our tracking indirect costs, I believe we should buy it.
At this moment in time, in the absence of a sufficient amount of data, we can only provide an approximation of the results.	Currently, without enough data, we can only approximate the results.

Despite the fact that the study team did not bother to do an analysis of the soil, the results give a fairly clear indication that the residue of uranium is present.	Although the study team neglected to analyze the soil, the results clearly indicate uranium residue.
The CEO gave a speech in a short span of time regarding the dutiful obligation a company has to the individuals who own shares of stock in it.	The CEO spoke briefly about a company's obligation to its shareholders.
In the event that the elevators are dysfunctional, proceed with an immediate contact of Building Maintenance.	If the elevators are not working, call Building Maintenance immediately.

Do not be brief at the expense of tone. Whenever establishing a friendly and personal tone is as important as the message, then longer and more conversational phrases are appropriate. In a memo whose purpose is to thank employees for an extraordinary effort, for example, a CEO might write, *I'd like to express my deepest appreciation for the long hours you've recently put in* rather than *Thank you for working overtime* or *Your dedication gratifies me.* These two are succinct but fail to convey any genuine sense of gratitude; because they are dispassionate, they preserve an impersonal separation between the writer and his readers. Maintaining that the longer sentence is "wordy" is a failure to understand both the purpose of such a statement and the nature of authentic communication—it is tantamount to arguing that music should be concise.

6. Avoid redundancy.

Remember the meanings of words. Because *history*, by definition, concerns only the past, the phrase *past history* is redundant; because *November* is a month, *the month of November* is redundant. In *Advance planning will enable us to completely avoid hidden pitfalls*, the writer is ignoring the definitions of *planning*, *avoid*, and *pitfall*. Don't say things that go without saying. Explicitly stating the implied words dilutes emphasis, complicates reading, wrecks the writer's credibility, and often misleads.

Ordinary speech teems with redundant expressions; their sheer familiarity seduces us into accepting them without question. But each time we read that someone wore a smile *on her face*, that someone has taken a leave *of absence*, or that someone has plans *for the future*, we are observing the vapor trail of a mind on autopilot. For those alert to redundancy, life is a never-ending journey through Wonderland, as signs declare, *This gate is locked to prevent entry* and *Unwanted trespassers will be prosecuted by the law*. When the guard comes to sort out the unwanted from the wanted trespassers, he is a *security guard*, and he does not merely arrive but *arrives on the scene*, and he does not arrive at midnight but at *twelve o'clock midnight*.

Respect definitions and let them do the work. Avoid such overlapping meanings as *specific example, advance warning, past experience, carefully scrutinize, postpone until later, completely destroyed,* and *whether or not*. Remember the understanding that the reader brings to the page, and cut every word that does not further understanding.

How to Test for Redundancy

Whether an expression is redundant depends on what the reader knows. What degree of expertise does the reader bring to the page? Does the reader know that 1993 is a year? If so, then such a phrase as *in the year 1993* is redundant, and *in 1993* will suffice. Does the reader know that when people nod, they nod *their heads in agreement* and when they shrug, they shrug *their shoulders*? If so, then *nod* and *shrug* will do. Every professional knows what an island is, so to point out that Mangareva is an island *entirely surrounded on all sides by water* is to add a flurry of syllables that melt before they add anything helpful.

Silly redundancies (*7 A.M. in the morning, including but not limited to,* and *a period of three weeks*) are easy to spot; all we need to do is remember definitions. But often the matter is far more subtle, and the writer must use discretion.

Consider the following sentence:

> Venezuela, a South American country, is a member of OPEC.

Is the phrase *a South American country* redundant? For some readers, it is; for other readers, it provides useful information. Arguing that people should know where Venezuela is gets the writer nowhere. If the reader doesn't know that Venezuela is in South America, then he doesn't know that Venezuela is in South America, and no degree of wishful thinking or academic bellyaching will change that. The practical question is this: Does the precise emphasis of my sentence depend on the reader's being reminded that Venezuela is in South America? Do most readers believe that OPEC consists entirely of countries in the Middle East? If so, then *a South American country* is a useful phrase.

Consider the following sentence:

> The onlookers were horrified when the space shuttle *Challenger* exploded.

Is the phrase *the space shuttle* redundant? That depends on what the reader knows. If all readers know that *Challenger* was a space shuttle, then the phrase is unnecessary and should be cut; if some readers don't know that *Challenger* was a space shuttle, and the writer's meaning depends on their knowing it, then the phrase is essential. Things that "go without saying" for some readers need to be said for other readers. Remember your audience's degree of expertise.

With the reader's expertise in mind, writers can avoid redundancy by (1) knowing the meaning of words and (2) asking this question: "as opposed to?" In *Additional financial funding is absolutely essential for the end completion of the project*, the writer who knows the meaning of *funding* should inquire of his adjective, "*Financial?* As opposed to some other kind of funding?" He should do this twice more in his sentence, looking at the meaning of *essential* and *completion* and challenging *absolutely* and *end*. In plain style, his meaning is concisely expressed as *Additional funding is essential for the completion of this project*.

Some redundant expressions send the mind lurching off into the realm of science fiction. *She is pregnant with a baby* and *Tattoos While U Wait* beg the questions of what else she might be pregnant with and whether U could ever leave an arm or a buttock behind, have it tattooed, and pick it up later. *With a baby*—as opposed to? *While U Wait*—as opposed to?

The Right Motive, the Wrong Technique

Writers sometimes commit redundancies from an honest motive—that of clarifying a word they believe their readers may not know. While this is decent behavior, it results from a misstep in word choice; explanations and clarifications will be unnecessary if the writer chooses words well in the first place.

Take, for example, the phrase *consensus of opinion*. One who writes this redundancy evidently believes that his readers don't know what *consensus* means. But if readers are unfamiliar with *consensus*, wouldn't it make more sense to respect the meanings of words and write *shared opinion*? After all, the purpose of the sentence isn't to expand the reader's vocabulary but merely to make a point.

If readers aren't familiar with a particular word, then it's best to use a different word. One who writes, *He fell and broke the humerus bone in his left arm* must assume that his readers don't know what a "humerus" is. (It is always a bone and always in the arm.) Readers who don't know what a humerus is may be edified to learn that it is a bone, but they still do not know which arm bone it is and, more to the point, increasing their vocabulary is not the goal of the sentence. *He fell and broke his left arm* would be tidy if that is all the writer means. If the precise location of the injury is important, then *He fell and broke his left arm between the elbow and the shoulder* would perform admirably. Readers do not need to encounter a "humerus" in order to get on with understanding.

Avoid redundant explanations of difficult words. Pick simple words in the first place. Rather than write the profoundly redundant *She experienced a sudden cardiac infarction of the heart*, it is better to say *She had a heart attack;* rather than write about *herbivorous dinosaurs that ate plants*, it is better to write about *plant-eating dinosaurs*.

Illogical Emphasis

In his excitement, the fighter pilot radios that the target was *totally destroyed;* in the heat of her impassioned speech, the politician declares that a bill would impose a *difficult hardship* on an industry. No one would argue that *totally destroyed* is unemphatic—but it is redundant, and *obliterated* captures the meaning in a word. In the same vein, *difficult* does promote the idea of hardship—but *difficult hardship* is redundant, and *the bill would cripple the industry* is far more emphatic. In emotional moments, few people bother to be exact in their choice of words. But business writing is an activity best done with a cool head. It's best to honor the meanings of words.

Consider the stop sign. In its succinctness, it epitomizes plain style. All it says is STOP. That's all it says because (1) that's all readers need and (2) STOP means "stop" without qualification (there are no degrees of stopping). If the sign read STOP COMPLETELY, it would be redundant; if it read STOP IN A THOROUGH MANNER BEFORE PROCEEDING, it would be absurd in its disrespect both for the meaning of words and for what the reader brings to the discourse. If it read ANY AND ALL PERSONS OPERATING A VEHICLE OF ANY DESCRIPTION FOR ANY PURPOSE WHATSOEVER ARE HEREBY ADVISED THAT A COMPLETE AND THOROUGH CESSATION OF FORWARD MOTION IS A LEGAL OBLIGATION BEFORE PROCEEDING IN AFOREMENTIONED VEHICLE THROUGH THIS INTERSECTION, it would have crashed the boundaries of the absurd, plunged down the rabbit hole, and wandered goggling—with other such writing ironically called legal—in the Zone Beyond Reason.

STOP is plain style. *Stop* means "stop." Nothing else is required; anything else would not merely be unnecessary but would beg the reader to find loopholes. Even *stop completely* is silly. But such phrases as *joint agreement* and *mutual cooperation* are just as silly—if you think about them. *I love you* is a handy thing to say to a loved one; *I currently love you* will not be as well-received.

Honor definitions and let them do the work. One who

writes *positive growth* has forgotten that his readers know what *growth* means; one who writes *foul stench* must think his readers are unable to catch a foul whiff from *stench*. A smell can be foul or pleasant, but a *stench* is always foul and an *aroma* is always pleasant. (Does *foul aroma* sound reasonable?) When you modify a word, make sure that the modifier contributes to clarity; modify only when you wish to indicate a degree.

Some things (like damage) occur in degrees. It is sensible to write *slightly damaged* or *heavily damaged*; it is equally sensible to write *recent experience* or *driving rain*. But it is preposterous to write *past experience, falling rain, depreciate in value, collaborate together, completely totaled, entirely surrounded,* or *utterly dead.* In the following sentences, the implied words have been crossed out.

> In ~~the month of~~ August ~~in the year~~ 1991, the Baltic States declared their ~~total and complete~~ independence from the Soviet Union.
>
> Because he is ~~a qualified~~ expert in ~~the area of~~ wetlands management, we have asked for him to ~~assist in~~ helping us write the Environmental Impact Statement ~~document~~.
>
> She was unsure whether ~~or not~~ to extend the ~~established~~ tradition of avoiding ~~the pronoun~~ *I* in business writing.
>
> Throughout the ~~entire past~~ history of Western civilization, ~~certain~~ specific tenets ~~and ideas~~ have been ~~basic~~ fundamental.
>
> Unless we base our forecast ~~for the future~~ on our ~~past~~ experience, we will prolong ~~the duration of~~ these ~~unfounded~~ rumors.

Thanks to their ~~joint~~ cooperation, the companies now enjoy many ~~positive and desirable~~ benefits.

We have decided to postpone ~~until a later time~~ adding any ~~additional confining~~ restrictions to the ESOP.

Our last invoice ~~for payment~~ has been ~~completely~~ ignored by the client, whose ~~utter~~ refusal to pay ~~funds~~ promptly ~~and in a timely manner still~~ remains ~~and continues to be~~ a serious ~~and unresolved~~ problem.

Upon ~~close~~ scrutiny, his ~~internal~~ memorandum regarding his leave ~~of absence seemed to suggest that he~~ implied that he was not given ~~adequate enough~~ time to recuperate ~~from his illness~~.

His ~~personal~~ opinion is that imports ~~from foreign countries~~ actually foster ~~positive~~ competition by American companies, but he ~~still~~ remains ~~diametrically~~ opposed to the ~~complete~~ elimination of ~~trade~~ import quotas.

When to Use *not un-* Constructions

The dishonest writer uses *not un-* constructions to avoid commitment or responsibility. He will tell you that a situation was *not unpredictable* (and leave it at that) to avoid saying that the thing was predictable and that he failed to do his job predicting it. This is yet another instance of bad faith, but it occurs so often that *not un-* has (like the innocent passive) become taboo in business writing.

Every construction in the language has its place. The honest writer (whose motto, in a nutshell, is "Do what works") uses a *not un-* construction in good faith whenever one is logically required. One is required when the writer's job is to refute the kind of contentions that sound like this:

Detecting the missiles with infrared alone is impossible.
The attorney is unlikely to file another appeal.

It is unusual for the species to be seen so far north.
The effects of the regulation were unforeseen.

If someone contends that a thing is *impractical,* common sense argues that the simple refutation is *not impractical.* Common sense, however, doesn't stop there. When you refute something, you are also obliged to assert something:

Detecting the missiles with infrared alone may be very difficult, but it is not impossible.
In fact, the attorney is not unlikely to file another appeal. We expect her to do so by the end of the week.
Despite Dr. Vork's claim, it is not unusual for the species to be seen so far north. Studies over the past twenty years confirm dozens of sightings as far north as Panama.
The effects of the regulation were not unforeseen. Several administrators vigorously opposed it, insisting that it would stifle competition.

Besides contributing to wordiness and ambiguity, *not* can spoil the tone of communication. Writers inadvertently lose readers—and businesses lose customers—with such sentences as *We will not process your claim at this time because you did not include the three estimates.* A civilized writer, who by definition empathizes with the reader, would recast that sentence so that it tells the reader something positive: *After we receive the three estimates, we will promptly process your claim.*

Use *not* whenever you must. Just make sure that no other word or phrasing will do. If an experiment *does not prove* something, it hardly *disproves* the thing (though it could *fail to prove*); if you are *not in favor* of a proposal, it is silly to *disfavor* it (though if you mean you *object* to it, you should write that).

In the sentences below, *not* and *not un-* constructions impair clarity. Note how the assertions in the examples on the right improve tone, clarify meaning, and foster simplicity.

We did not choose to continue the project.	We chose to end the project.
It is not infrequent that the project manager does not accurately estimate costs.	The project manager frequently underestimates costs.
They did not remember that they were not supposed to lock the emergency door.	They forgot to leave the emergency door unlocked.
The jury did not take all of the evidence into consideration and was not able to reach a verdict.	The jury overlooked some of the evidence and was unable to reach a verdict.
He does not believe in the existence of quarks.	He doubts that quarks exist. *or* He refutes the existence of quarks. *or* He denies the existence of quarks.
The language of the regulation is not precise and not consistent, and therefore the meaning is not clear.	The language of the regulation is imprecise and inconsistent, and therefore the meaning is unclear.
It is not unlikely that the agency will not neglect to send another squad.	The agency will probably send another squad.
It is not unusual for them not to be in full and complete compliance with EPA regulations.	They often fail to comply completely with EPA regulations.
We are not of the belief that the software has undergone insufficient testing.	We believe that the software has been adequately tested.
This report intentionally does not include information whose source has not been verified.	This report excludes information from unverified sources.
It is not improbable that they were not unaware of the radioactive spill.	We believe they knew about the radioactive spill.

The proposal is not acceptable because it does not take our schedule into consideration.	The proposal is unacceptable because it disregards our schedule.
It is not out of the question that they will not fail to market the product before we do.	They may be able to market the product before we do.
The committee did not succeed in its attempt to make the amendment not part of the bill.	The committee failed to exclude the amendment.
The regulation does not exclude all trade with Haiti.	The regulation permits some trade with Haiti.

7. Avoid unnecessary repetition.

"Never repeat words" is another of the false taboos that undermine good writing. Repetition often works. In fact, repeating a word or phrase is a fine idea as long as you repeat for effect. A writer at an electric utility, attempting to convince the developer of a shopping mall to choose electricity (rather than oil or gas) for heating and air-conditioning, uses good judgment when she writes,

> Using electricity will result in lower installation costs, lower maintenance costs, and lower fuel costs over the life of the structure.

Because the idea of *lower* is what the writer wishes to emphasize, the reader encounters the word three times. This is effective writing. The alternative sentence below, in which *lower* appears only once, is much less emphatic and persuasive.

> Using electricity will lower not only your installation costs, but also your maintenance costs and fuel costs over the life of the structure.

The trick is to avoid *unnecessary* repetition (i.e., repetition that calls attention to itself or dilutes emphasis because it does not serve to hammer home a point). *HUD issued RFQ G91207 on December 10. HUD's RFQ G91207 sought bids from contractors interested in presenting writing workshops for HUD* is a typical example of unnecessary repetition. All that the writer needed to say was this:

> On December 10, HUD issued RFQ G91207, which sought bids from contractors interested in presenting writing workshops.

Another example of senseless repetition: *The Cost/Benefit Analysis (C/BA) performed in March indicates that additional regulation would serve no useful purpose. There is a strong suggestion from the March C/BA that additional regulation would actually impede productivity by increasing the paperwork burden on small business.* All that the writer needed to say (all that the reader needs) is this:

> The Cost/Benefit Analysis performed in March indicates that additional regulation would serve no purpose. The analysis strongly suggests that the additional paperwork would merely decrease productivity.

Don't forget what the reader already knows. This forgetfulness is what accounts for the unnecessary repetition of words and phrases. Repeat only for effect. If the branch has already been identified as *Special Operations branch*, the budget has already been characterized as *the proposed FY94 budget*, and the only project mentioned is the *White Winds project*, then repeating those ideas does nothing but clutter the sentence:

> Any cuts to the proposed FY94 budget of the Special Operations branch would force us to eliminate several programs crucial to the White Winds project.

On Being Emphatic

In any sentence, the order of the words largely determines meaning and emphasis. An imprecise order of words opens the door to unintended meanings and magnificent madness. Which of the following (clear) sentences presents the reader with a cannibalistic attorney and carrion-consuming biologists?

It was said that his client was eaten alive by the defense attorney.	The defense attorney remarked that his client was "eaten alive."
Because they consume carrion as well as kill their own prey, some biologists regard lions as scavengers.	Because lions eat carrion as well as kill their own prey, some biologists regard them as scavengers.

The order of words will foster clarity or foment ambiguity. Note the ambiguity in the following sentences on the left; note how moving a word clarifies the expression.

People whose work requires travel frequently become depressed.

Frequently, people whose work requires travel become depressed.
or
People whose work requires frequent travel become depressed.

Reporting the discovery immediately will create chaos in the scientific community.

Reporting the discovery will immediately create chaos in the scientific community.
or
Immediately reporting the discovery will create chaos in the scientific community.

On Being Emphatic

The order of words will either simplify or complicate reading. In which column below are the sentences easier to understand?

The policy, as it is now written, is, according to the ACLU, unconstitutional and, if enforced, will, when challenged, for the first time, in court, be declared null, void, and illegal.	According to the ACLU, the current policy is unconstitutional and will be declared illegal the first time it is challenged in court.
The economic consequences of forcing small businesses to provide comprehensive medical insurance to all employees are currently unknown.	We do not know the economic consequences of requiring small businesses to provide comprehensive medical insurance to all employees.

The order of the words suggests the intended emphasis. Note how the sentences in the right column better emphasize the annual nature of the adjustment and the urgency of the need.

The cost-of-living index is adjusted on an annual basis by the Commerce Department.	Annually, the Commerce Department adjusts the cost-of-living index.
The errors must be immediately corrected.	The errors must be corrected immediately.

The beginnings and endings of sentences are emphatic. Below, in the examples on the left, both *auditor* and *second quarter of 1993* are deemphasized. The idea of *auditor* is presented as part of an extra phrase, and *second-quarter 1993* is presented as an adjective. If you wish to stress the auditor and the second quarter of 1993, then those ideas must be moved to positions of emphasis. In the revisions on the right, *auditor* becomes the subject, and *second quarter of 1993* ends the sentence.

The risk, according to the auditor, is minimal.	The auditor believes that the risk is minimal.
We have not received the second-quarter 1993 tax report.	We have not received the tax report for the second quarter of 1993.

You reduce emphasis on an idea when you place it in the middle of a sentence. Below, in the examples on the left, *the last five years* and *relevant* are heavily emphasized. Note how placing these ideas in the middle of the sentences makes them seem less important.

For the last five years, our principal goal has been to improve customer service.	Our principal goal over the last five years has been to improve customer service.
We must stress that the idea is relevant.	We must stress the relevance of the idea.

The order of words takes the place of vocal emphasis. Because the reader doesn't know how you'd stress the words if you were speaking, she relies on their order for a sense of their relative importance. And she reads what you write. If you were speaking, you might stress *yesterday* in such a sentence as *We only received your RFP yesterday*. But the reader doesn't hear that, and if your intent is to express how recently you received the RFP, then you write, *We received the RFP only yesterday.*

Writing for results requires that you (1) decide what you're writing about, (2) find the right word for it, (3) use that word as the subject, and (4) tell the truth in simple language. The truth is contained in the verb. Find the precise verb and reveal it as soon as you can.

Remember Technique 4. Don't worry about whether your sentence is active or passive. Do concern yourself with whether you are emphasizing the idea you intend to emphasize. (The reader assumes you've chosen the subject deliberately.) In the example below, if you wish to stress Professor Landris, you will have an active sentence; if you wish to stress what she discovered, you will have a passive one.

Active	Passive
Professor Landris discovered a complete skeleton of *Allosaurus*.	A complete skeleton of *Allosaurus* was discovered by Professor Landris.

Regardless of whether the resulting sentence is active or passive, pick the precise verb and reveal it. Nothing more frustrates understanding than verbs that are "politely late" to the party. Always organize sentences so that the verb appears as close as possible to the subject.

The techniques that follow will make your writing emphatic.

8. Put words in subject-verb-object order.

The subject-verb-object order of words stresses the right idea, fosters simplicity, and minimizes errors in grammar. If the subject acts, this order of words also improves economy. Below, in the example on the left, the subject (*wolf*) and the verb (*thrives*) are widely separated; the passive construction *endangered by scientists* is not what the writer wishes to convey (nor does he wish to convey that the scientists endangered the wolf several years ago). In the revision, subjects and verbs are side by side; as a result, there are no unintended meanings and the expression is easier to follow. Note that the revision requires two sentences.

The red wolf, thought to be endangered by scientists several years ago in coastal North Carolina, today thrives there.	Several years ago, scientists thought that the red wolf was endangered in coastal North Carolina. Today it thrives there.

Remember, a sentence can be both "correct" and difficult to understand. The goal of a good writer is to write sentences that are correct and clear on the first reading; the subject-verb-object order of words helps make them easy to understand. Below (on the left) are some common constructions that create needless complexity.

Avoid putting a lot of words between the subject and verb. Instead, place the verb as close as possible to the subject, as in the examples on the right.

- Several benefits from the new policy permitting employees to work out of their homes will accrue to us.

    Several benefits will result from the new policy permitting employees to work at home.

- The ultimate breadth and extent of the toxic spill in the Fairfield area that occurred last week has not yet been determined.

    We have not yet determined the ultimate extent of the toxic spill that occurred last week in the Fairfield area.

- We will, in the event that premiums for medical insurance continue to skyrocket as they have over the last decade, convert to an HMO.

    If medical insurance premiums continue to skyrocket, we will convert to an HMO.

- The opportunities for multiple breakthroughs in the field of hydrodynamic research related to energy production increase annually.

    In the field of hydrodynamic research related to energy production, opportunities for multiple breakthroughs increase annually.

Refrain from "funhouse" structures, where the writer's "discoveries" jump out at every turn. Minimize punctuation by organizing more deliberately.

- The benefits, to my way of thinking, of establishing an office in Italy are manifold.

    I believe that we would benefit in many ways from establishing an office in Italy.

- This option, unlike the others, will enable us, on a monthly basis, to track our direct costs.

    Unlike the other options, this one will enable us to track our direct costs each month.

The CEO, along with the president, is of the opinion that the restructuring, as it is now planned, will increase profitability.	Both the CEO and the president believe that the planned restructuring will increase profits.

Let people do things. Many of the problems in emphasis, clarity, and conciseness will disappear if you let people (and things) act.

	[*Is Dr. Putkus a volatile fellow?*]
Many fears have been raised regarding the possibility of an eruption by Dr. Putkus.	Dr. Putkus has often expressed concerns about the possibility of an eruption.
	[*Note how economy improves.*]
It is our finding that there was no other option for Mission Control except to abort the launch.	We find that Mission Control had no option but to abort the launch.
	[*But the report was not racing.*]
Racing to meet the deadline, the report was sent by overnight express.	Racing to meet the deadline, we sent the report by overnight express.
	[*Clearances aren't considered for positions.*]
To be considered for the position, a top-secret clearance must be obtained.	To be considered for the position, you must obtain a top-secret clearance.

Rather than write lengthy sentences where nothing in particular is emphasized, be willing to give each important idea a sentence of its own. All adults have heard "rules" regarding the maximum length of sentences—twenty words or fewer, fifteen words or fewer—and these should be discarded. They are artificial; some sentences require thirty, forty, or fifty words.

Let emphasis dictate length. Think of an art gallery where one small picture hangs on a large white wall. What would happen to the emphasis on that picture if another were placed beside it? What would happen if two more were added?

["Improved productivity" lost.]
Our new headquarters building, which is scheduled to be completed next year, will enable us to provide each employee with a private office, which should significantly improve productivity.

["Improved productivity" rescued.]
When we move into our new headquarters building next year, each employee will have a private office. As a result, productivity should improve significantly.

[This requires two readings.]
The results of the survey among managers that was conducted to determine the relationship of dollars spent on training to improved productivity last month are summarized below.

[This requires only one reading.]
Last month we surveyed managers to determine the correlation between training dollars and productivity. This report summarizes the results of the survey.

Sentence length is purely a matter of judgment. Just understand the practical consequences of what you do. Length dilutes. Brevity emphasizes.

[One sentence, perfectly "correct," but nothing in particular emphasized.]
Wordiness, jargon, and pretentious language have been creeping into our letters and memos, and this is not good for business, and I want it immediately to stop.

[Three sentences, each idea emphasized.]
Wordiness, jargon, and pretentious language have been creeping into our letters and memos. Such writing hurts business. It must stop immediately.

9. Place modifiers precisely.

In English, the meaning of an expression depends largely on the order of the words. There is a vast difference, after all, between the following sentences.

We saw a film about preventing explosions in the conference room.	In the conference room, we saw a film about preventing explosions.
After being convicted of embezzlement, the defense attorney said he and his client would probably appeal.	After his client was convicted of embezzlement, the defense attorney said they would probably appeal.
On her own time, she has been acting as a mentally ill advocate.	On her own time, she has been acting as an advocate for the mentally ill.
I saw the rare lemur staring at the moon with my own eyes.	With my own eyes, I saw the rare lemur staring at the moon.

Meaning isn't the only thing at stake. A well-organized sentence will be read and understood effortlessly; a haphazard order of words obstructs sense and requires too much effort from the reader. Sentences like the ones below require several readings because modifying phrases have been spewed out and left to rot where they landed.

> He discovered the technique in Switzerland that we use to separate molecules by accident forty years ago.
> She claimed that she was singled out for abuse from January through April by her manager without reason.
> We must insist that you pay the invoice for the shipment that we mailed on October 19 by December 1.

Make sure that each modifying expression relates unequivocally to the word you intend it to describe. Organize the words so that each modifier appears right beside the word it describes. When modifiers are loosely placed, ambiguity results:

> The consultant has been trying to get us to extend his contract for two months.

Because the phrase *for two months* has been carelessly placed, the sentence has three (equally plausible) interpretations:

> For two months, the consultant has been asking us to extend his contract.
> The consultant is requesting a two-month extension to his contract.
> The consultant is asking us to extend his two-month contract.

The next few pages will alert you to the common ways in which modifiers cause confusion, ambiguity, and difficulty. The solution to each problem is the same—place the modifier beside the word you intend it to describe.

- Modifiers that begin sentences bear careful watching. Everyone has encountered the bizarre images that result when modifiers "dangle." (The one in the sentence below describes a very enthusiastic repairman.)

> Spitting sparks and whipping wildly from side to side, the repairman attempted to reconnect the downed power line.

When you begin a sentence with a modifying phrase, make certain that the next idea is what you intend that phrase to modify.

Hurrying through the report, an important detail was overlooked by the auditor.	[*The auditor, not the detail, hurried through the report.*] Hurrying through the report, the auditor overlooked an important detail.
Because they can lift fifty times their weight, biologists regard the ants as the strongest of all animals.	[*Few biologists are so impressive.*] Because ants can lift fifty times their weight, biologists regard them as the strongest of all animals.
Flying at 40,000 feet, the missile silos were impossible to detect.	[*Missile silos never behave in this manner.*] From 40,000 feet, we could not detect the missile silos.

On Being Emphatic

After being planted in the Rose Garden, the First Lady called the bush "a small piece of England."	[*The First Lady wasn't planted in the Rose Garden. The bush was.*] After the bush was planted in the Rose Garden, the First Lady called it "a small piece of England."
While lethal in large doses, the study suggests that the drug may be beneficial in small doses.	[*Truly, some studies are lethal in large doses, but the lethality here should apply to the drug.*] The study suggests that the drug—while lethal in large doses—may be beneficial in small doses.
Unlike most manned space vehicles, the chief engineer claims that the AVR-20 can remain in orbitation mode for one full year.	[*The chief engineer may or may not be gratified by such a comparison.*] The chief engineer claims that the AVR-20 (unlike most manned space vehicles) can remain in orbit for one full year.
Screaming their slogans at one another, the police dispersed the opposing protesters.	[*The protesters were the ones screaming.*] Screaming their slogans at one another, the opposing protesters were dispersed by the police.
Reeling from a series of setbacks, the regulators called the company "a financial basket case."	[*But the regulators were not reeling.*] The company is reeling from a series of setbacks; regulators have called it "a financial basket case."

- Modifiers that end sentences bear careful watching. More often than not, phrases that end sentences are merely "tacked on" and can be understood to relate to two (or more) ideas. Observe the unintended meanings and ambiguities in the sentences in the left column; note that each revision either entirely rewrites the expression or places the modifier right beside the appropriate word.

Serious allegations have been raised regarding sexual harassment by Professor Hill.	[*Professor Hill raised the allegations.*] Professor Hill has raised serious allegations regarding sexual harassment.

We demanded their commitment to pull their troops out of Kuwait by noon on Saturday.	[*We did not intend to demand that the Iraqis remove their troops by a certain time, but that they commit by a certain time.*] We demanded that they commit, by noon on Saturday, to pull their troops out of Kuwait.
He wrote that the satellite must have fallen into the ocean in his report.	[*The report contained no ocean.*] In his report, he wrote that the satellite must have fallen into the ocean.
When we checked the files, we found records of employees that were out of date.	[*The employees aren't out of date.*] When we checked the files, we found out-of-date records of employees.
We saw the Bigfoot looking at us through high-powered binoculars.	[*And no doubt the Bigfoot was chuckling.*] Through high-powered binoculars, we saw the Bigfoot looking at us.
You can see our new headquarters building driving up Interstate 270.	[*Should you be careful not to blink?*] From I-270, you can see our new headquarters building.
Many items are stored in the warehouse of great historical significance.	[*The warehouse itself isn't that important.*] Many items of great historical significance are stored in the warehouse.
Old floppy disks will be collected by secretaries of every size.	[*Why is the size of the secretaries relevant?*] Secretaries will collect old floppy disks of every size.
We watched the space shuttle lift off from the observation bunker.	[*It must have been a warming experience.*] From the observation bunker, we watched the space shuttle lift off.
They warned us that competition would be stiff at the outset.	[*But true competition remains stiff.*] At the outset, they warned us that competition would be stiff.

- Often, a modifier in the middle of a sentence is ambiguous because it can relate to the idea that precedes it or to the one that follows it. The alert (i.e., sensible and deliberate) writer places each prepositional phrase where it belongs. Observe how the capricious placement of phrases in the examples in the left column can make simple thoughts sound like something overheard in the Twilight Zone.

He was stung by the parking lot on the left side of his neck.	Near the parking lot, he was stung on the left side of his neck.
There was never any reason in his mind to hesitate.	In his mind, there was never any reason to hesitate.
She never thought she'd be promoted to vice president in her wildest dreams.	In her wildest dreams, she never thought she'd be promoted to vice president.
The top-secret files are on the desk in his briefcase.	The top-secret files are in his briefcase on the desk.
This stock in her opinion will double in two years.	In her opinion, this stock will double in two years.
The FTC believes this advertising in several ways to be unfair.	The FTC believes this advertising is unfair in several ways.
Our goal for ten years has been to simplify writing.	For ten years, our goal has been to simplify writing. *or* Our ten-year goal has been to simplify writing.
Simplifying the procedure soon will save us thousands of dollars.	By simplifying the procedure soon, we will save thousands of dollars. *or* Simplifying the procedure will soon save us thousands of dollars.
Their remarkable record in such ventures of success is due to hard work.	Their remarkable record of success in such ventures is due to hard work. *or* Hard work accounts for their remarkable record of success in such ventures.

She states that lewd comments were made by the watercooler on the way down the hall.	She states that she heard lewd comments as she passed the watercooler.
Their plan to increase hydroelectric output in any event will prove costly.	In any event, their plan to increase hydroelectric output will prove costly.
Our revenue forecast for six months has been undergoing revision.	For six months, we have been revising our revenue forecast. *or* We have been revising our six-month revenue forecast.

- *Which* clauses bear careful watching. Place each *which* clause right beside the word it actually describes. Loose placements can result in wild ideas like those in the left column.

The new policy will begin next year, which has been approved by the board of directors.	[*"Next year" does not require approval from the board.*] The new policy, which will begin next year, has been approved by the board of directors.
We learned a technique in the training we attended last week, which will prove useful.	[*"Technique," not "week," will prove useful.*] We learned a useful technique in last week's training.
The Senate blames the stalemate on the House, which shows no signs of being resolved.	[*"No signs of being resolved" applies to "stalemate."*] The Senate blames the House for the stalemate, which shows no signs of being resolved.
Biologists report seeing snow leopards in the Himalayas, which they believed were extinct years ago.	[*The Himalayas are in no danger of extinction.*] Biologists report seeing snow leopards (which were believed to be extinct years ago) in the Himalayas.

On Being Emphatic

- *That* clauses also bear careful watching. Like other modifying phrases, a *that* clause must be placed right beside the word it describes.

The investment was ill-advised that they made in robotics.	The investment that they made in robotics was ill-advised. *Better:* Their investment in robotics was ill-advised.
Several remarks were made by the engineer that we found surprising.	The engineer made several remarks that we found surprising. *Better:* The engineer made several surprising remarks.
They plan to take several measures in the coming year that will immunize them against fluctuations in interest rates.	Next year they plan to take several measures that will protect them from fluctuations in interest rates.
Numerous errors were made by the company in its proposal that claims it believes in "excellence."	The company that claims it believes in "excellence" made numerous errors in its proposal.

- *Only, even,* and *just* bear careful watching. These three words, like hoboes, tend to wander around and camp wherever they choose. For the sake of precision, place them right before the idea you intend them to modify.

The expression:	logically means:
I only watch football on Sundays.	I don't do anything else on Sundays.
I watch football only on Sundays.	I don't watch football on any other day.
I watch only football on Sundays.	I don't watch anything else on Sundays.
We only requested the arbitration yesterday.	We merely requested (not demanded) it.
We requested the arbitration only yesterday.	It's been only one day since our request.

Smoking is only allowed in designated areas.	It's not "encouraged" or "advised."
Smoking is allowed only in designated areas.	It's allowed nowhere else.
We only decided to renovate the executive lounge.	We merely decided to do it, as opposed to signing a contract.
We decided to renovate only the executive lounge.	We decided to renovate the lounge and to renovate nothing else.
The prosecution's only evidence is circumstantial.	The prosecution has but one bit of evidence, which happens to be circumstantial.
The prosecution's evidence is only circumstantial.	All of the prosecution's evidence is circumstantial.
The CEO was not even aware of the lawsuit.	He didn't know about it.
The CEO was unaware even of the lawsuit.	He was unaware of a lot of other things.
Even the CEO was unaware of the lawsuit.	This is surprising (since he, of all people, should be aware of it).
It's frightening even to contemplate a slight decrease in revenue.	The mere act of contemplating this prospect is frightening.
It's frightening to contemplate even a slight decrease in revenue.	Any decrease in revenue, no matter how slight, is a frightening prospect.
The species was even observed mating underwater.	Someone actually saw this; in other words, it isn't myth or hearsay.
The species was observed mating even underwater.	The insatiable species mates underwater, as well as on land.
The bank protested even the positive findings of the audit.	Besides protesting the negative findings, the bank protested the positive ones.
The bank even protested the positive findings of the audit.	The bank did not merely complain, but went so far as to protest the findings.

On Being Emphatic

We've just received the proposal.	We recently received it.
We've received just the proposal.	We've received only the proposal, not the necessary supporting documents.
Dr. Coombs wrote just the report.	That's all she wrote.
Dr. Coombs just wrote the report.	She merely wrote (not edited) the report. *or* She recently completed the report.

- *Either . . . or* and *neither . . . nor* expressions also bear careful watching. When these words are out of balance, the reader has to read the sentence twice. The problem is typified by the following sentence:

> Either the FDIC must raise funds or reduce the extent of insurance coverage.

When the reader encounters *Either the FDIC*, he expects the *or* phrase to suggest another organization—*Either the FDIC or the RTC* must do thus-and-such. Instead, the sentence compares the FDIC to the act of reducing. In this sentence, the writer intends to balance *raise* and *reduce*:

> The FDIC must either raise funds or reduce the extent of insurance coverage.

The technique is simple and consistent: Place *either* (or *neither*) immediately before the word you intend to compare; place *or* (or *nor*) immediately before the word compared. The examples in the left column are imprecise; the revised sentences are precise.

Either they overlooked the deadline or ignored it.	They either overlooked the deadline or ignored it.

Expenses must either be reduced or revenue must be increased.	We must either reduce expenses or increase revenue.
The company can neither explain the cost overrun nor the delay.	The company can explain neither the cost overrun nor the delay.
The report neither contains all the relevant data nor the most current data.	This report contains neither all the relevant data nor the most current data.
Either we change our policy or risk being censured for violating EEO regulations.	Either we change our policy or we risk being censured for violating EEO regulations. *or* We either change our policy or risk being censured for violating EEO regulations.
The species is either extinct or it exists now only in inaccessible locales.	The species is either extinct or exists now only in inaccessible locales.
They neither accepted the apology nor the offer of settlement.	They accepted neither the apology nor the offer of settlement.
Either the Senate will take up the issue or it will be taken up in the House.	Either the Senate or the House will take up the issue.

10. Hyphenate to create the appropriate emphasis.

Because readers pay particular attention to the way a sentence starts and concludes, any word in these positions receives a natural emphasis, or "weight." It's as though a bright spotlight shines on the idea that ends a sentence—and the practical writer will not end a sentence arbitrarily. She will be deliberate and end with the word that deserves emphasis. Consider the sentence below.

The executives have gone on a retreat that will last for four days.

On Being Emphatic

That's an emphatic sentence if the writer wishes to emphasize *executives* and *four days*. But it isn't an emphatic sentence if she wishes to emphasize *executives* and *retreat*. *Retreat* is buried and thus receives very little stress. If the writer wishes to highlight *retreat*, then she needs to place that word in the spotlight at the end of the sentence—and knowing how to hyphenate enables her to.

The executives have gone on a four-day retreat.

As you read the examples below, notice how a word's importance is magnified when that word appears at the end of the sentence. Notice also that we hyphenate when the word precedes the noun. All of the sentences are "correct." The question is: How precisely does the order of words capture and present the writer's intended emphasis? Only the writer can answer that—but she should know the technique that will give her both options.

[*Emphasizes "long term."*]
They plan to establish a partnership that will extend over the long term.

[*Emphasizes "high income."*]
The new taxes are aimed at professionals who earn a high income.

[*Emphasizes "end of the year."*]
Enclosed is a copy of our analysis for the end of the year.

[*Emphasizes "none too robust."*]
The latest statistics indicate a recovery that is none too robust.

[*Emphasizes "your own pocket."*]
The new plan will reduce the expenses you pay out of your own pocket.

[*Emphasizes "partnership."*]
They plan to establish a long-term partnership.

[*Emphasizes "professionals."*]
The new taxes are aimed at high-income professionals.

[*Emphasizes "analysis."*]
Enclosed is a copy of our end-of-year analysis.

[*Emphasizes "recovery."*]
The latest statistics indicate a none-too-robust recovery.

[*Emphasizes "expenses."*]
The new plan will reduce your out-of-pocket expenses.

Hyphenating also enables the writer to avoid suggesting something she doesn't intend. In *We were delighted by the forecast for six months,* the delight probably didn't last for half a year: We were delighted by the *six-month forecast.* In *His manager has been urging him to take a vacation for three weeks,* either the manager has been urging for three weeks or the manager has been urging him to take a *three-week vacation.*

As useful as it is, the hyphen is notoriously misunderstood and prone to abuse. When the special of the day is half of a baked chicken, but the menu says *half-baked chicken,* the restaurateur will marvel at the brisk sale of beef; when the owner of a burned-out store is captioned, on the television news, as a *burned-out storeowner,* viewers will wonder what his need for a vacation has to do with the arson they've been hearing about.

What the Hyphen Does

The hyphen connects things. It can (1) connect prefixes to words (*re-sign, anti-inflammatory, pro-choice*) to form a different word and (2) connect words to form a single noun (the *president-elect,* a state of *self-consciousness*) or a single verb. Guidance on these usages is available in dictionaries and style guides. We are concerned here with the third major use of the hyphen—the one that requires the writer's judgment as she invents compound adjectives ("unit modifiers") on the spot.

Consider, for example, the position of the writer who has written, *Executives have responded favorably to the new format, which is easy to scan.* She had ended her sentence with—and has therefore emphasized—an afterthought (the parenthetical *which is easy to scan*). Her sentence is perfectly correct. But let's suppose she wishes to emphasize *format*. She knows that it's the writer's job to direct the reader's understanding, and thus she needs to change the order of the words. So she writes, *Executives have responded favorably to the new, easy-to-scan format.*

You won't find *easy-to-scan* in any dictionary or style guide. For flexibility—the flexibility that enables a writer to emphasize the right idea—an understanding of technique is crucial.

How to Use the Hyphen

Consider the following sentence:

We need to reassess our goals for the third quarter.

The words are in normal parts-of-speech order: *Third* is an adjective and *quarter* is a noun (as they ordinarily are), and thus no hyphen is required. If the writer wishes to emphasize *the third quarter*, then this is a fine expression. But if the writer wishes to emphasize *goals*, then she will have to alter the order of words and write, *We need to reassess our third-quarter goals.*

When we write the words in that order, we have changed the way *third* and *quarter* are behaving: *Quarter* is no longer a noun. It has been wrenched out of its traditional role and has become part of an adjective modifying *goals*. The hyphen is used to indicate that in this sentence *third-quarter* is a unit.

It's the same principle over and over. When you have a phrase like *a suspension of five days,* you can convert it to *a five-day suspension.* When wondering whether to hyphenate, just ask yourself, "Is it a five suspension *and* a day suspension?" Clearly, it isn't. *Five-day* is a unit of thought. Those two words are behaving like a single adjective, and they come before the noun. And so you hyphenate.

In another example, we have *boosters that use solid fuel.* In that phrase, *fuel* is a noun and *solid* is an adjective. If we convert the phrase to *solid-fuel boosters,* we've altered the way *fuel* behaves in the sentence; it's now part of an adjective. We hyphenate because they are not "solid" boosters *and* "fuel" boosters.

Here we have *adjustments to reflect the cost of living,* and the phrase can become *cost-of-living adjustments.* We hyphenate *cost-of-living* because the three words are behaving like an adjective. We aren't talking about "cost" adjustments, "of" adjustments, *and* "living" adjustments.

And here we have *records that are out of date.* That's fine, but if we wish to emphasize *records,* we write *out-of-date records.* They aren't "out" records, "of" records, *and* "date" records. And so we hyphenate the phrase.

That's basically all there is to it. Our *capability for verifying intelligence* becomes our *intelligence-verifying capability.* An Olympic sprint of 100 meters becomes a *100-meter dash,* a cup that holds 4 ounces becomes a *4-ounce cup,* and a beam that is 6 feet long becomes a *6-foot beam* (it isn't a "6" beam *and* a "foot" beam). Diskettes with a high density are *high-density diskettes,* objectives for the near term are *near-term objectives,* and an organization that is strapped for cash is a *cash-strapped organization.* Bonds that are rated AAA become *AAA-rated bonds;* a dog that can detect explosives by sniffing becomes an *explosive-sniffing dog*—not, we hope, an explosive sniffing one.

Follow Accepted Usage

The hyphen connects words to indicate that they form a unit, and writers need to hyphenate only when the reader wouldn't instantly recognize the words to be a unit. There's no need to hyphenate *law enforcement* officer or *federal budget* deficit because those phrases are so commonly seen that they are understood to form units. Readers recognize *life insurance* company, *long distance* bill, and *atomic energy* program; hyphens do not aid clarity in familiar phrases and may safely be omitted.

11. Keep equal ideas "parallel."

When ideas are of equal importance, a sentence should express them in identical structures. Consider, for example, the following (difficult) sentence:

> We arrived on the site, interviewed the supervisor, and it is thought that the work will be completed on schedule.

Besides being awkward, that sentence is ambiguous. Who's doing the thinking—the writer or the supervisor? Since the sentence begins with two verb constructions (arrived, interviewed), we make the last idea fit the pattern by finding a third verb:

>   1   2   3
> We arrived on the site, interviewed the supervisor, and determined that the work will be completed on schedule.

If the ideas below were on an old-fashioned scale, would they balance?

> It is far more prudent to invest the dividend than distributing it.

The ideas of investing and distributing are expressed in different ways in that sentence. Since they are being directly compared, they should appear in identical structures:

It is far more prudent to invest the dividend than to distribute it.
or
Investing the dividend is far more prudent than distributing it.

- When you compare two or more ideas, make sure that the ideas are comparably presented, as they are in the examples on the right.

We have neither received the final report nor the interim findings.	We have received neither the final report nor the interim findings.
They are not opening an office in London but in Edinburgh.	They are opening an office not in London but in Edinburgh.
Not only was the training practical, but it was relevant.	The training was not only practical but relevant.
They are not only concerned about imports but about fluctuations in the value of the dollar.	They are concerned not only about imports but about fluctuations in the value of the dollar.
The companies have both agreed to the merger and reorganization.	The companies have agreed both to the merger and to the reorganization. *or* The companies have agreed to both the merger and the reorganization.
We have both decided to reduce indirect costs and direct costs.	We have decided to reduce both direct and indirect costs.

- When you list ideas of equal importance, keep the ideas parallel, as they are in the right column.

[*These three nouns should not be parallel.*]	[*"Support to" is made parallel.*]
The hot line provides support to those suffering from addiction, their families, and friends.	The hot line provides support not only to those suffering from addiction, but also to their families and friends.

On Being Emphatic

[*Two nouns and a conditional phrase.*]

We are concerned about relevance, validity, and whether the testimony is credible.

[*One infinitive, one "-ing" verb, and a noun.*]

Careful analysis of the photographs is necessary to detect troops, for verifying the placement of reserves, and the identification of movement.

[*Capricious shifting from passive to active forces the reader to wonder whether "we" are responsible for all three activities.*]

The issue must be defined, we must research it, and a report on the matter must be produced as soon as possible.

[*Two prepositional phrases and a noun phrase.*]

You are to be commended for your diligence, for your compassion, and the professional manner in which you handled the difficult situation.

[*One infinitive and a noun phrase.*]

To foster a professional image and for the improvement of customer service, we are installing an 800 number.

[*One simple verb and one "-ing" verb.*]

Problems in clarity will be minimized if you write with verbs and by paying attention to the order of words.

[*Three nouns, if all apply to "evidence."*]

We are concerned about the relevance, validity, and credibility of the evidence.

[*Three infinitives.*]

Analyze the photographs carefully to detect troops, to verify the placement of reserves, and to identify movement.

[*Three verbs, if "we" must do all three.*]

As soon as possible, we must define, research, and report on the issue.

[*Three nouns.*]

You are to be commended for your diligence, compassion, and professionalism in this difficult situation.

[*Two infinitives.*]

To foster a professional image and to improve customer service, we are installing an 800 number.

[*Two simple verbs.*]

You will minimize problems in clarity if you write with verbs and pay attention to the order of words.

[One infinitive and one "-ing" verb.]
The purposes of the trip were to see the effects of the bombardment firsthand and assessing the extent of the damage.

[Two infinitives.]
The purposes of the trip were to see the effects of the bombardment firsthand and to assess the extent of the damage.

[One "-ing" verb and one infinitive.]
The project superintendent's responsibilities include writing a weekly report and to ensure that the work is on schedule.

[Two "-ing" verbs.]
The project superintendent's responsibilities include writing a weekly report and ensuring that the work is on schedule.

[One preposition and one noun.]
Inside each of us is something worth expression and necessary to be expressed.

[Two precise verbs.]
Inside each of us is something that both deserves and demands expression.

- Some ideas do not belong in parallel structures. The capricious "cramming in" of ideas can suggest a meaning other than the one you intend. In the sentence below, did the regulators say one thing, or both?

> The regulators stated that the company took unfair advantage of its market position, and we have a good chance to win if we sue.

Some readers will assume (naturally enough) that the regulators said both things; others will assume that the regulators said only the first thing and that the writer then expresses his own opinion.

If the regulators said both things, then the ideas should be made parallel:

> The regulators stated that the company took unfair advantage of its market position and that we have a good chance to win if we sue.

If the regulators said only the first thing, then the meaning requires two sentences:

The regulators stated that the company took unfair advantage of its market position. We have a good chance to win if we sue.

Here are some additional examples.

[*Did the biologist say one thing, or both?*]
The biologist said that the animal was believed to be extinct, but it has been seen recently in the Kenyala Forest.

[*If the biologist said both things.*]
The biologist said that the animal was believed to be extinct but that it has been seen recently in the Kenyala Forest.

[*If the biologist said only the first thing, then the meaning requires two sentences.*]
The biologist said that the animal was believed to be extinct. It has, however, been seen recently in the Kenyala Forest.

[*Does the contract stipulate both things?*]
The contract stipulates that we must supply the materials, and we must ship them within thirty days.

[*If the contract stipulates both.*]
The contract stipulates that we must supply and ship the materials within thirty days.

[*If the contract stipulates only the first thing, then the expression requires two sentences.*]
The contract stipulates that we must supply the materials. If we are to meet our timetable, we must ship the materials within thirty days.

Remember also that in a sea of ideas, emphasis always drowns. When you decide that an idea deserves emphasis, put it in a separate sentence.

[What the reader reads is crammed into one unemphatic sentence.]	[What the writer means requires two sentences.]
After interviewing the applicants, we decided to increase the salary level of the position and to offer it to Dr. Struthers.	After interviewing the applicants, we decided to increase the salary level of the position. Only by doing so can we attract Dr. Struthers, the most qualified candidate.
["Before you leave" cannot live in the same atmosphere as "when you arrive."]	[These ideas require separate sentences for both clarity and emphasis.]
When you arrive at the facility, make sure to show your identification, sign in, go immediately to the briefing room, and secure all classified materials before you leave.	When you arrive, show your identification, sign in, and go immediately to the briefing room. Be sure to secure all classified materials before you leave.

12. Do not allow dogmatic folderol to interfere with plain style.

Do not let nonsense parading as "rules" interfere with clarity and simplicity. This language of ours is a wonderful instrument, capable of infinite precision and subtlety. But merely that—merely capable. Writers who tread in the minefield of "don'ts" (e.g., Don't split an infinitive, Don't end a sentence with a preposition, Don't repeat words, Don't let inanimate objects do things) will find needless complexity exploding at every step.

In the United States, there is no consistency in the way English is taught. Teachers disagree about what usages are "proper" and "improper." In seventh grade, Johnny learns never to start a sentence with *because*; in eighth grade, he learns it's okay to start a sentence with *because*, but never ever to start with *so*. In high school, he learns never to use parentheses; in college, he learns never to use dashes, but to use parentheses. At work, his manager (who attended the same college but had a different instructor for Composition 101) insists that parentheses are never necessary, that *contact* isn't a verb, and that *however* must always be followed by a comma.

It's hardly surprising that Johnny (now John) lacks confidence and hates to write. So does his manager. So does the executive vice president. Everyone has been subjected to a chaos of contradictory rights and wrongs, goods and bads, propers and impropers. Sometimes it's miraculous that anything gets written at all.

We live, alas, in an imperfect world, and there will always be readers who snort with righteous annoyance when they spot a split infinitive or a sentence fragment. Some readers will snort about exclamation points; others will snort about single-sentence paragraphs. Any reader who is a die-hard pedant will find *something* to snort at. You never know what will make a reader snort, so it's best not to worry about it. We must let these readers snort. Nothing good comes of humoring them. The majority of readers wish merely to understand.

Here is where our thinking should begin: In business, practical communication is what counts. The question is not what Sister Louise said twenty-five years ago, or what Miss Thompson said in ninth grade, or what Assistant Professor Jones said in freshman composition class. The question is this: What works?

On Choosing Words

In a single sentence, Ben Franklin summed up the wisdom involved in choosing words. He didn't write, "Lexical decisions resulting in the arcane are decidedly inferior to aforesaid decisions resulting in the mundane." He could have written it that way (he certainly knew all those words), but he didn't. Ben was a clear thinker, and he knew that unusual words obstruct understanding. Because he wanted people to understand him, he wrote, "Never use a longer word when a shorter word will do."

The good writer won't quibble with that. He won't fiddle with the definition of *shorter* and pretend that since *nexus* has only two syllables, it's a "short-enough" word. If he's writing to a general audience, he'll use *link*. He won't pump helium into his link and release it to waft into the reader's mind as *linkage*. He'll use *link*.

He'll use *link* as a verb or a noun, depending on what he chooses to emphasize. He might write, for example, "How are the two issues linked?" He might write, "I see no link between the two issues." But he'd never use *linkage* as a verb, committing something like, "We must linkage the issues." And he would never, unless he wishes to amuse himself, use *nexus* as a verb, which would result in a sentence like, "Diplomats from the two countries are attempting to nexus the issues." He won't clap a verb-sounding ending onto *nexus* and come up with *nexify* or *nexusize*. He's a good writer, not a nitwit. He'll use *link*.

What's interesting about Franklin's remark is that it's phrased as an edict. Ben didn't bother to explain why shorter words are better than longer ones because he assumed that the common sense in his remark is self-evident. But Franklin was a child of the Enlightenment, and he believed that "Reason" would always be recognized as such. It isn't.

When we scorn little words—when everyday words don't seem "good enough"—we open the door to complexity and sometimes to disaster. A writer at a federal agency, wishing to describe a professional position, meant to say, "This position requires MC&G certification." He could have used those words, but he did not. He reversed Franklin's axiom and didn't use a shorter word when he could hallucinate a longer one, and this is what he wrote:

> This position is encumbered by a qualified MC&G professional.

It's easy to trace what happened here. The writer knew something (but not nearly enough) about the word *incumbent*, tried to make a verb of it, misspelled it, and ended up with *encumbered*. He wrote a clear sentence that is not remotely related to what he meant. And he did this because, to him, ordinary words were "unprofessional."

Writing for results begins here: The words we use must never impose an artificial complexity on an idea. "Artificial" is the key. Things are complicated enough without our creating a veneer of needless complication. The beauty of accepting this is that it gives us freedom to write simply: *Combat emplacement evacuator* reverts to *shovel* and *taking a proactive position* reverts to *act*. If a writer does not accept it—if he insists on using *utilize* where the sense is simply *use*—then writing for results stands no chance. Don't open the door to complexity. It's always out there, snorting and pawing the ground, waiting for its moment in the china shop.

Nowhere in this book will you find *ameliorate* used in battle, though *improve* is used a lot. Nowhere in this book will you find *elucidate* doing the work of *clarify*. I respect your intelligence, and I believe that you know the longer words, but I also believe that *clarify* is clearer on first reading than *elucidate*. I believe that the distinction between *ameliorate* and *improve* is so minor that it makes no sense to use *ameliorate*. I think I would be a bad writer if I wrote something like, *To ameliorate your writing, elucidate the relationships between periodic expressions.* That's inflated style. What I want to say is complicated enough—and because that's so, you benefit when I write it this way: *To improve your writing, clarify the relationships between sentences.* That's writing for results.

Maybe you've noticed that those frightening "English teacher" words—*gerund, participle, correlative conjunction, subjunctive, imperative,* and so on—appear nowhere in this book. If I know my audience, those terms are impractical: Not only do they fail to convey anything, but they provoke nightmarish associations and memories. I know that your eyes would glaze over if I wrote something like, *A coordinating conjunction is preceded by a comma when it connects independent clauses.* Mine would glaze over if I had to read something like that. And it seems to me that glazed-over eyes signal bad writing.

The elucidation of one's intention has its locus in the selection of the elements of diction is an eye-glazing-over way of saying, in writing for results, *Clarity starts with the choice of words.* Give yourself permission to use ordinary words. Clarity will follow.

How to Find the Right Words

People frequently complain that they have trouble finding the words for an idea. Everyone who's ever tried to write has experienced the same difficulty: "I know what I mean, but I can't seem to put it on paper."

This trouble stems from one (or more) of three sources. First, it's quite possible that we *don't* know what we mean. The idea may not be a clear one after all—we never know whether any idea is clear until we see it on the page, and we might need to concentrate a bit more or examine the rough idea from several angles before the thought itself crystallizes for us. Second, we may be able to *sense* the right words but be unable to call them forth; they tease and tantalize in the back of the mind, flirting with the forebrain but refusing to reveal themselves. This is a matter of our employing those words infrequently, so that they're not part of the "active" vocabulary. To overcome this problem, all that is necessary is a larger vocabulary, a facility with words. Finally, we sometimes simply don't like the way a clear idea sounds. This is a dark impulse, the ogre in the writer's spirit. It is a matter not of having little facility with words, but of having little respect for them and little concern for the reader. The ogre snares a perfectly lucid expression like *As we agreed, the contract amount has been increased by $100,000* and "professionalizes" it into *Per agreement, subject contract funding terms have been adjusted upward in an amount not to exceed $100,000.*

The ogre vanishes in a little puff of smoke when you butt him with a hard head. That happens somewhere on the mystic plane. In the tangible world, the other two difficulties in finding words can be overcome with practice. Here are some suggestions: *Develop a practical vocabulary.* Note the word *practical*. While nothing's wrong with having *arride* and *nuque* in your vocabulary, when will you ever have occasion to use them outside a game of Scrabble or a crossword puzzle? It makes much more sense to know the shades of meanings of everyday words.

Consider the varieties of *looking*. A scientist *observes*, an editor *scrutinizes*, the EPA *monitors*, the FBI and the CIA *surveille*, an angry person *glares*, a surprised person *stares*, a very surprised person *gapes*, and a person beyond gaping *gawks*. We *watch, ogle, gaze, view, review, oversee, rubberneck, leer, squint, admire, glance, overlook, glimpse, peer,* and *peek*—and all these words convey something different. A crop can be in some way damaged, or it can be *stunted, withered, wilted,* or *shriveled*; a policy can positively affect sales, or it can *buoy, increase, boost,* or *stimulate* them. Must you write *initiate*? Are you truly *initiating*, or actually *beginning* or *starting*? And even if professionals in your field use *initiate* to describe the precise origination of something, will the reader of *this* sentence partake of the same distinction? If all the reader wants to know is when something began, then *began* will do perfectly well, and *initiate* will be excessive. Collect and use the practical words.

• *Know the meanings of the words you use every day.* If you do, you'll use *utilize* only when you've been ingenious in your use of something (you might utilize this book as a doorstop, for example). You'll use *expect* when an outcome is definite (a pregnant woman expects a baby); you'll use *anticipate* when the outcome is less definite (she anticipates the date of birth).

Respecting the precise definitions of words enables the writer to convey subtle distinctions and shades of meaning. Not respecting them creates confusion, but it enables the writer to show off. For people who wish to show off, every *repetitive* becomes a *redundant*, every *define* becomes a *definitize*, and every *unclear* becomes an *ambiguous*. What some writers fail to recognize is that the longer words are not precise synonyms for the shorter ones.

Ambiguous, for example, is not necessarily a synonym for *unclear*. *Ambiguous* has a precise meaning and denotes a particular problem with clarity (that an expression has two or more logical meanings); *unclear* might mean merely "vague," but it could mean "confusing," "muddled," "cloudy," "murky," or even "deceptive." And for every *unclear* that erroneously becomes an *ambiguous*, we have an *outline* puffing up into a *delineation*, a *fire* exploding into a *conflagration*, a simple *method* ballooning into a *methodology*, and a *granting immunity* whooping into an *immunize*. (This enables us to immunize witnesses without breaking the skin.)

Learn the shades of distinction inherent in the words of everyday writing—the difference between *delay* and *postpone*, the difference between *we have often requested* and *we have repeatedly requested*, the difference between *we anxiously await your response* and *we eagerly await your response*. The everyday words are the practical words to know.

- *Read.* Writers who rarely read cannot reasonably expect to develop a sense of the nuances of words. You do not need to read voraciously, or even every day, but you do need to read—a newspaper, a magazine article, a novel, *something* other than the memos and reports that lurch through the halls of business and government. What's important to understand is that "organizational" writing tends to inbreed, with the same results as those when people inbreed: Certain traits, not always good ones, become exaggerated.

Read with a critical eye. When do good writers use

leave? When do they use *depart*? When do they use *proportion*, and when *percentage*? You'll learn that *likely* is most often used as an adjective (an outcome is likely) and that *probably* is an adverb (something will probably happen). You'll notice that there is a world of difference between *enable* and *allow*, between *prohibit* and *forbid*, and between *if* and *whether*. In a good newspaper, you'll find *insure* used only in the context of insurance, *assure* used when the sense is person-to-person (the CEO assured the stockholders of something), and *ensure* for every other sense of "make certain" (we need to ensure that our product is safe). Such distinctions are the ones worth knowing, and you'll learn them if you read. Watch your source; read well-written material. A supermarket tabloid may do more harm than good.

- *Visualize.* Use your imagination to "see" the action. If you want to indicate that two wires should be connected and made into one, you could use *attach together* or *connect together*, but if you visualize it, you'll find *splice*. If you remember and visualize a time when you *did not bother to*, you'll find *neglected*; if you visualize a time when you *did not take something into consideration*, you'll find *overlooked, disregarded,* or *ignored*. Visualize it. Are you *attaching* or merely *enclosing* something? Did the executives truly *discuss* the contract, or did they *debate* or *argue* about it? Did they *squabble, bicker, dispute*? Which word best captures the truth? When employees have paper to recycle, do they put it into a *container*, or into a *box*, a *bin*, a *tray*, or a *can*? Is this document a *contract*, a *proposal*, a *memo*, an *analysis*, a *report*, an *article*, a *pamphlet*, a *brochure*, an *announcement*, a *newsletter*, an *invoice*, or a *monograph*?

- *Demand precision from yourself.* When we write about concrete things—about bricks, trucks, and butterfly bolts—

conveying ideas is difficult enough. Unfortunately, much of business writing is necessarily abstract (we write more about intangible things like *customer satisfaction* and *rule-making procedures* than we do about physical bricks). And in the domain of abstractions, choosing precise words becomes imperative. Call things by their right names.

Select your nouns with care. Is the right word *statute* or *regulation*? Is the right word *policy* or *procedure*? In business, individual customers receive *bills*, and organizations receive *invoices*. Sellers charge a *price*; buyers think in terms of *cost*. Be especially exact in your choice of verbs. A launch can be *delayed*, or it can be *postponed indefinitely*, *canceled*, or *aborted*. If you demand precision, you'll never write, *The SEC's ruling will impact sales*. Instead, you'll use a precise verb: The ruling will *increase*, *decrease*, *complicate*, *jeopardize*, *boost*, *cripple*, *stimulate*, *simplify*, *ensure*, or do something else in particular to sales.

- *Trust yourself.* If the sense you wish to convey is "Opening an office in San Diego would be impractical," then go ahead and write that. Why look for another way to put it? If you look for a "better" way to say it, the sentence will inflate into something on the order of *At this point in time, the establishment of a San Diego regional facility would not seem to be a prudent or viable goal*. Somewhere in that flurry of syllables is your plain idea; your original words expressed it best. If you want to convey that "Customers are complaining that our bills are difficult to understand," then use those words. They're good ones. Don't pump the idea full of anabolic steroids so that it reads, *The majority of our clientele have recently voiced discomfort with our invoicing documents, claiming that these documents are difficult to comprehend*. Just write your original sentence. Trust yourself.

If you have a clear thought, chances are 100 percent that it is packaged in clear words. If the idea is clear, all you need to do is give yourself permission to write it that way. In workshops, I sometimes ask writers to pick a word that best captures a sense. I might, for example, ask them to select the best word for the sense of "rare" from the list below:

rare
unusual
strange
unique
uncommon

Many writers pause to think about the matter. Some select *strange* or *unique*. I point out that the word for *rare* is *rare*, just as the word for *policy* is *policy* and the word for *must* is *must*. You can't out-think the definitions of words. The eyes light up. Could it truly be that easy? Of course it can! And unless the writer is complicating things, it ought to be just that easy.

We extend this reasoning to entire sentences. Someone at the FDA, intending to convey that *Currently, we are unsure whether aspartame is dangerous*, once wrote, *Aspartame is potentially dangerous*. Most people, aware of how the FDA determines whether a substance is dangerous, assume that the sentence means "Aspartame is dangerous if you consume a large amount of it." This is another thought entirely, but it is the one most apparent in that sentence.

I ask writers a simple question: If the writer wishes to let readers know that *Currently, we are unsure whether aspartame is dangerous*, then what are the words for that thought? "Those words," someone will say. "Those exact words." And she'll be right. False teeth are false teeth, and if

Mr. Smith ordered a set of false teeth, then the way to say it is *Mr. Smith ordered a set of false teeth*, not *A full complement of compensated edentia was requisitioned by Mr. Smith.* Writers with a taste for the bizarre and the baroque are encouraged to become diplomats, stand-up comedians, or high-level politicians. Rare words sparkle everywhere in these professions, where the meaning of a statement isn't as important as its immediate effect.

Some Common Problems With Ordinary Words

A number of very good books explain the distinction between pairs of words like *less* and *fewer*, *insure* and *ensure*, and *whether* and *if*. The words discussed here complicate understanding even though they are "correct." They are listed in order of their potential to create mischief:

- Avoid relying on *affect* or *impact* as verbs. They are correct, but they never convey anything in particular. If you mean that the new software will increase productivity, then don't write, *The new software will affect productivity.* Use *increase* as the verb. If you mean that a report boosted consumers' confidence, then say that. Avoid writing, *The report impacted consumer confidence.* It is wishful thinking to believe that *positively impact* and *negatively impact* are better; they are wordy as well as imprecise. If you mean *stimulate* and *jeopardize*, say so. The reader reads the words, not the mind.

- Avoid *shall*, a notoriously ambiguous word that can indicate either *will* or *must*. In a sentence such as *The contractor shall fully document all indirect costs*, the word *shall* can be interpreted to mean that the contractor intends to (will) document indirect costs or that the contractor is legally obligated to (must) document indirect costs. Writers who mean *must* are strongly encouraged to write *must*. Writers who wish to indicate a future tense are strongly encouraged to write *will*.

- Be careful with *may*. Incautious use of this word leads to ambiguity, as in *The auditors may photocopy all records*. Does this mean that the auditors have authority to photocopy, or that they possibly will photocopy? In the former case, use *are authorized to*; in the latter case, use *might*.

- Use *this, that, these,* and *those* to refer to previously mentioned topics. Substitute them for the horribly intrusive *said, above, abovementioned,* and the grotesque *heretofore-abovementioned*. After you introduce a contract, refer to it as *this contract*, or *the contract*, not *the abovementioned contract*. When you're referring to more than one contract, write *these contracts*, not *said contracts* or *the above contracts*. That's what *this* and *these* are for.

- In memos, avoid referring to the issue in the SUBJECT line as *subject* issue or *captioned* issue. Doing so interrupts the flow of reading because it yanks the reader back to the top of the page. For example, if the subject line reads *ODM contract terms*, don't begin the memo with the phrase *Subject contract*. Instead, write a civilized expression: *We need to clarify several terms in our contract with ODM*.

- Challenge the verb *support;* look instead for the precise verb. *Support* is vague. In *These findings support the conclusion that*, the findings could *indicate, prove, underscore, reveal, imply, verify, confirm, suggest,* or *demonstrate*. In *We can support our sales force by improving customer service*, the meaning is simply *help* or *assist*. When one writes, *The company supports employee participation in*, one could mean that the company *encourages, endorses, funds, simplifies,* or even *mandates.* Challenge this word each time you use it.

• Beware of *potentially.* The word is often redundant, frequently confused with *probably,* and repeatedly misleading when used to indicate a lack of certainty. Taken at face value, *potentially dangerous* and *potentially hazardous* are redundant (*dangerous* and *hazardous* indicate the potential for harm). In *The new advertising is potentially misleading,* the writer intends to indicate either some degree of probability or a lack of certainty. *The new advertising could (might, will probably) mislead our customers* would do in the former case. In the latter case, write *We are unsure whether the advertising is accurate.*

• Don't generalize about *-ize* words. A secretary of commerce once wrote a memo in which he forcefully admonished his writers never to use any word that ends in *-ize.* This admonition, which stemmed from his frustration with *prioritize,* robbed writers of some very useful words: *Maximize, minimize, sanitize,* and *scrutinize,* for example, are all simple. Writers at the Commerce Department found that they could no longer simply *realize* something but had to *be of the realization that.* Common sense argues that there is a gulf of difference between a common word like *terrorize* and mind-boggling, spur-of-the-moment inventions like *incentivize* ("motivate," "convince," "persuade," "entice," "encourage"), *functionalize* (a hallucinatory word that means "open," "complete," or "prepare"), *orientize* (just say "orient" or "acquaint"), and *diminize* ("reduce" would perform admirably). Our language is leaping with verbs. Find the right one.

• Avoid transparent, clichéd euphemisms such as *this office, this company,* and *this organization.* When the reference is clear, just write *we*. Sentences such as *This office is in receipt of your letter* are instantly translated into *We have received your letter.* The reader should not need to translate her own language. When you need to say *I*, don't write, *this writer, this office, this desk, this author,* or any other phony substitute. Write *I*. That's what the word is for. Anything else is needless complication.

• Whenever possible, avoid euphemisms. Most euphemisms suggest bad faith. The famous *unintended impact with the ground* (airplane crash), *revenue enhancements* (tax increases), and *collateral damage* (damage to nonmilitary targets in war) spring from the writer's belief that he can cloak an unpleasant truth in vague or abstract words. This practice backfires. Readers are not fooled for long, and when they grasp the plain meaning, they realize the writer's attempt to deceive.

• Minimize your use of "legal-sounding" terms. *Heretofore* is a chuckleheaded way to write *previously. Herein* and *herewith* are nearly always redundant (*herein enclosed is* means "enclosed is"). *Pursuant to our discussion* usually means "as we discussed" or "as a follow-up to our discussion." In ordinary English, *henceforth, hereafter,* and *hereinafter* mean "from now on." In plain style, the dwarfs *therein* and *wherein* mean nothing more than "there" and "where," respectively. Besides complicating the text, such words destroy tone, rendering the writing mercilessly cold.

Shun archaic words. The word for *two times* is *twice,* but to indicate *three times* you need to write *three times. Thrice* is outmoded and calls attention to itself, just as *beseech* and *behoove* are outmoded and distracting. *It would behoove us to reduce our price* was a grand expression in 1618, but these days *We need to reduce our price* is more effective. *Betwixt and between* may seem like a saucy phrase the first time you hear it, but *between* will suffice. *Wherefore* takes people to the balcony scene in *Romeo and Juliet*—as pleasant interlude, perhaps, but hardly a desirable detour in a contract. Just write *why*. Use reasonable contemporary words.

• Use extreme caution when importing foreign words and phrases. Readers might be familiar with *vis-à-vis*, but why take the chance? Use *about* or *regarding*. Only if all of your intended readers know French will *élan* give your sentence a dash of *je ne sais quoi*. Lovely Italian words like *pentimento* and *glissando*, as mellifluous as they are, belong to the arts and are best confined there. If you must discuss *bubei* (a Japanese word meaning "regretful contempt for America"), then define the word when you introduce it. Phrases from Latin are particularly obnoxious to most readers, and writers (including attorneys who write to a general audience) are strongly encouraged to stop baffling the rest of us with such mysterious remarks as *in re, pro se, res ipsa loquitur,* and *inter alia*. The writer may know what these phrases mean, but that is never the point. It's best to write in English.

• Be careful with jargon. Jargon (technical terms unique to a profession) is useful shorthand when it remains within the confines of a specific priesthood. When it escapes those confines—when readers do not belong to the priesthood—it is as incomprehensible as any foreign language. The strangely enticing phrase *charismatic megafauna* means "lions, tigers, and bears" to people at the EPA, but *lions, tigers, bears, and other large animals* would prevent most readers from guessing. Telecommunications engineers can bandy *uplinks, downlinks,* and *transponders* back and forth to one another with great success, but the general audience needs those terms defined (a diagram wouldn't hurt). In computerese, *an AI appli-*

cation presupposes RAM, datalinks propagate, and *modules migrate.* Every word has its place, and those are fine in the community of computer experts. But for the general audience they are profanely absurd—just as the English teacher's *imperative indicative* is absurd when it is launched at the tender ears of seventh graders. Readers may not need to encounter the technical terms in order to get on with understanding.

• Use careful judgment when you introduce acronyms and abbreviations. If your readers are familiar with *ATM*, then you needn't clutter the text by formally introducing the abbreviation, as in *For your convenience, we are installing an Automated Teller Machine (ATM).* Common abbreviations require no explanation. Unfamiliar ones do. If your intended readers will not instantly recognize *BARF* to stand for the "Best Available Retrofit Facility," then common courtesy suggests that you spell the name and then introduce the abbreviation. But don't introduce *BARF* merely for the sake of introducing it. When you introduce an abbreviation, do so because you'll need to refer to it at least once more (and fairly soon) in the document. Unless you have occasion to use the abbreviation again, introducing it is nothing but clutter. Be alert to wishful thinking. Some accountants believe that *K* means "thousands" and *M* means "millions." Other accountants read *M* as *thousands,* believing that if you meant *millions* you would write *MM.* If you have the least suspicion that the reader may not share your intended meaning for an abbreviation, then specify what you mean by it.

• Know how to use *i.e.* and *e.g.* The device *i.e.* means "that is" or "in other words." Use it to paraphrase, clarify, or point out something about the previous expression, and introduce it with parentheses: *Human error contributed to* the accident at Chernobyl (i.e., the technology was only partly to blame). The device *e.g.* means "for example" and is also introduced with parentheses: *Smoking has been banned in many common areas (e.g., hallways, lounges, and the cafeteria).* Writers are forever confusing these devices, and often with serious implications. In *Contractor agrees to replace defaulting items (i.e., fuses and bulbs) for two years from the installation date,* the contractor is liable only for the fuses and the bulbs. The writer intended to supply examples of items, but *i.e.* does not supply examples. It paraphrases what the writer meant by *items.* Practical sense argues that the phrases *for example* and *that is* are good ones to use; they are less likely to be confused.

- Be careful with *a* and *an*. The use of *a* and *an* has nothing to do with vowels and consonants. Use *a* before a consonant sound and *an* before a vowel sound. It is *a unique* solution, *a one-time* adjustment, *a European* office; it is *an MX* missile, *an FDIC-insured* account, *an hourly* rate.

- Honor connotations. Their product is *cheap,* but ours is *affordable.* They are *timid;* we are *prudent.* They may be *stubborn, inflexible, dogmatic, obstinate, obdurate,* or *muleheaded,* but we are *firm.* Pay attention to the echoes and associations of words. A client can be *late* paying an invoice, or he can be *delinquent.* In most businesses, it's better to *serve* customers than to *service* them.

- Don't terrify the reader with *be advised that.* By convention, this phrase is used to introduce something that the reader is not going to like very much: *Be advised that we are investigating allegations concerning your conduct, Be advised that your property taxes will increase, Be advised that the reduction in revenue will necessitate layoffs.* Reserve your use of this phrase for those occasions when the matter is truly serious. When the news is positive or neutral, write, *Please note that* or *Note that* instead.

- Beware of unintentionally insulting the reader with *for your information*. The phrase *for your information* has become forever linked with the defensive sense of "You're wrong, pal, and I'm about to straighten things out." When the bank falsely accuses you of failing to pay your mortgage on time, you respond, with justifiable annoyance, "For your information, the check cleared ten days ago." If you do not intend to convey indignation, substitute a precise phrase. *For your information, we are enclosing our brochure* could easily become *The enclosed brochure will acquaint you with our capabilities.* If you wish to indicate that no action is required, use *FYI*. While those letters "stand for" *for your information*, their practical effect is to convey "this is information only."

- Beware of *obviously*. Numerous relationships have been sunk by this torpedo of a word, which in effect calls the reader a dunce for not knowing what the writer, in his wisdom, already knows. *Obviously, you don't understand the complexities of the research* is degrading in the extreme. *It's obvious that funding this project would be a waste of money* is a bullying statement—the sort people resort to when they have no evidence to support their point and must rely on brawn alone. *The advantages of our product are obvious* will backfire. Words are cheap. Give the reader credit for having some intelligence. Lead her to that conclusion, but allow her to draw it.

- Avoid writing like a robot. The thrill of such phrases as *per our telecom, input appreciated,* and *receipt is noted* wears off very quickly for human readers. Plain style requires not that you write precisely as you speak, but that what you write might actually issue from the mouth of a sane, sensible, sober, awake, and reasonably courteous person. If you'd feel strange saying what you've written—if people would look askance at you and take a step away—then what you've written needs to be simplified.

- Avoid wrenching nouns into verbs. Rather than *dialogue* with people, it's simpler to *meet, talk,* or *confer* with them. Rather than *reference* something, just *refer* to it. *Memorandum all employees* is a grotesque way of saying *Write a memo to all employees*. Such a sentence as *They informationed us that the tremors had subsided* is a sadly comic way of saying they *told* us or *informed* us. Nouns are very good at being nouns, but they fall woefully short of the stamina required of verbs.

- Refrain from coining words. *Unsave* happened one day when a writer couldn't think of another way to say that he intended to *erase, delete,* or *dump* data from a file. *Incent* happened one day when a writer wished to shorten *incentivize*, which occurred one day when another writer couldn't find a way to say *motivate, entice, encourage, persuade,* or *convince*. The inclination to clap an *-ize* onto the backside of a noun is especially strong in bureaucracies: *quantity* becomes *quanticize* ("count"), *liquid* becomes *liquidize* ("melt"), and *arson* becomes *arsonize* (as in *Security now believes that someone arsonized the plant*). Marketing calls are not glorified but merely dandified when they are referred to as marketing *outdials;* calls from customers need not be tarted up into *customer indials*. And while it may seem logical for *prepone* to be the opposite of *postpone*, such a sentence as *Next week's meeting has been preponed to tomorrow* is little more than evidence of a frustrated comedian. Use ordinary words for ordinary things.

- When you must name something (e.g., a project, study, or device), give it a clear and logical name. *Functional*

Illiteracy is an impressive title for a report, but what does it mean? Is illiteracy in some way functional? Is someone functional even though he's classified as illiterate? Can someone barely function *because* he's illiterate? No one knows. An *Elderly Care Program* has nothing to do with care that is elderly, but is concerned with *Caring for the Elderly*. Don't be brief at the expense of your meaning. A *homeless advocate* is an advocate without a home, just as a *handicapped activist* is an activist who is handicapped. If you mean one who is an advocate for the homeless, say so; if you mean an activist for the handicapped, say so. Referring to boots as *leather personnel carriers* (the Army shortens this to LPCs) and to a telephone as a *telephonic communications instrument* is utter madness. Those things already have names.

- Challenge the everyday jargon of business. *Implement* and *institute* are vague words, sometimes intended as "adopt" and sometimes as "carry out" or "put into practice." In *We implemented the policy last year*, the reader is at sea. *Prioritize* is a hideous word masking the much simpler "rank," as in *The executives met to discuss and prioritize corporate goals*. Another problem with *prioritize* is that it lays eggs, and what hatches from those eggs are phrases like *performed a prioritization of*. Shiny, newly minted terms are especially seductive and require extra restraint. Like will-o'-the-wisps leading the unwary into quicksand, *build-down, negrowth,* and *downsize* have an allure fatal to simplicity and clarity. It is better to "dismantle something" than to *effect a build-down* of it, better to say that the economy "is shrinking" than to say it is *experiencing negrowth,* and far more courageous and humane to say "reduce the number of employees" than to say *downsize*.

- Avoid clichés. When phrases are cheapened through too-frequent use, they lose their power to ignite in the reader's imagination. Empty phrases like *state-of-the-art, few and far between,* and *once-in-a-lifetime opportunity* are little more than collections of syllables, husks from which the cicadas have flown. Rubber-stamp expressions such as *We are in receipt of your letter of March 19* and *Feel free to call me if you have any questions* make things easy for the writer—but because the reader encounters them a hundred times a year, they are little more than background noise. Those sentences are useful in that they enable the writer to get on and off the page with no effort, and they are perfectly appropriate in cases where acknowledgment is merely a formality. But in cases where sincerity is important, hunt for the right words, not for the ready-made expressions.

- Resist the temptation to exaggerate. Tell the truth instead. *Technical errors infest the proposal* is concise, but if there are only a few errors, then *infest* is inaccurate and reveals more about the writer's mood than about the fact. Avoid "crying wolf" with words. Don't write that something was *devastated, destroyed, obliterated,* or *annihilated* when actually it was damaged. Reserve *catastrophe* and *disaster* for situations that are truly catastrophic and disastrous, and refrain from using them to characterize every least inconvenience. Superlatives such as *excellent, outstanding,* and *superior* are like gold coins and should be spent sparingly; when the ordinary becomes excellent, "excellence" has lost its meaning.

- Stay abreast of the language; remain aware of how words are actually used. Words are in constant turmoil and evolution, and the meaning of a word—the only meaning that matters—is the one in your reader's mind. Every dictionary says that *peruse* means "to read thoroughly," but everyone I ask thinks the word means "to skim." Who's right? That's the wrong question. The right question is: What does the word truly convey to the reader? *Skim* and *scan* are clear words; *read thoroughly* is a clear phrase. *Peruse* begs misunderstanding.

If we follow the principles of derivation, *biannual* should mean "every two years" (*bi* + *annual*). But that doesn't stop precisely half of your readers from assuming it means "twice per year," that *biweekly* means "twice per week," and that *subsequent to* means "before," "because," or "as a result of." Ultimately, what the dictionary says doesn't matter, not in the moment of reading. We all wish for an authority somewhere, someone who lives on a mountain, who would have the final say on what a word means and how the word should be used. But there is no such person—and even if there were, people would bicker with her. The best we can do is to pick the words we're sure will convey what we mean, use those words and no others, and say what we have to say with a minimum of fuss and bother. That's writing for results.

Part Three
Practical Punctuation

Preliminary Remarks

Punctuation has a single purpose: To clarify the writer's intended meaning. If a good writer has a bias about punctuation, that bias leads him to use less, not more.

Two general principles govern the use of all punctuation. First, if a mark does not clarify the text, it should be omitted. Second, in the choice and placement of punctuation marks, the only goal should be to clarify the writer's precise meaning and emphasis.

The way punctuation is taught in this country might fairly be termed haphazard. Most adult Americans can remember hearing a teacher saying *Put in a comma where you'd take a breath,* and *Don't use a comma if you use an "and."* The truth is that the writer's breathing patterns have nothing to do with the way a particular sentence is punctuated. And while the comma does replace the "and" in a series of adjectives, it certainly doesn't do that in a series of nouns.

To be sure, there are a few inexplicable conventions writers must follow when punctuating. Why, for example, must a period always go inside quotation marks? No one knows. But that is the standard in America, and good writers deviate from the standards at their peril. Readers who know the standards expect the writer to adhere to those standards. When such readers spot an error, they stop reading and begin to proofread for more.

The section entitled Precepts suggests some ways to *think* about punctuation. The right thinking simplifies any task, and it's important to think accurately if we are to understand when, whether, and how to punctuate.

The few "English teacher" terms that simplify the discussion are introduced and explained in the section called Definitions.

Precepts

The way we think about a task will either simplify or complicate that task—and because punctuation is complicated enough, it's very important that writers think clearly about it. Here are some important things to keep in mind. With these ideas influencing the way you think about punctuation, you'll find that your judgment improves.

1. Punctuation cannot rescue sense from nonsense.

Before you punctuate, make sure (1) you've used the right words and (2) you've put the words in a sensible order. If the words aren't well chosen and well organized, punctuation won't help. In *Hurtling through the night sky, she saw a strange blue light*, punctuation is perfect, and she is the one hurtling through the night sky. In *In her affidavit, plaintiff contends she was touched on several occasions by the watercooler*, punctuation is excellent, and the watercooler is misbehaving. In the fabulously bizarre *Esskay hot dogs not only smell better when cooking, but they taste better when eating*, punctuation is perfect, and the hot dogs are both cooking something and eating something. In *All of these results are not valid*, no punctuation is required—and the sentence will be ambiguous anyway. (Are all of the results invalid, or only some of them?)

Punctuation is an after-the-fact aid to clarity. If the writer uses words that the reader doesn't understand—if he writes something like *Etymology fails to elucidate contemporaneous lexical utility*—punctuation will not help. If the writer creates long and convoluted sentences, punctuation may be precise, yet the reader may still have to read each sentence ten times to understand it. Punctuation has its limits, and expecting punctuation to clarify a loose, ramshackle structure of words is like expecting a coat of paint to shore up a dilapidated house. The paint won't do that, regardless of the skill of the painter. Only if the walls are in good shape will the paint make much of a difference. The practical painter prepares the walls; the practical writer puts the right words in the right order.

Understand the limits of what punctuation can accomplish. Do first things first: Put the right words in the right order, keep sentences relatively brief, and use words the reader understands. Only after these things are done can punctuation make a difference.

2. Punctuation retards the reading.

The primary reasons for punctuating are to clarify and separate ideas, but punctuation has an inescapable side effect: It slows the reading. Commas, semicolons, and parentheses are like barbed wire strung across the reader's path, and he must slow down to avoid impaling himself. Punctuate when you must, but try to minimize the need to punctuate. The way to do that is to write straightforward sentences. For example, rather than write *Elizabeth, undetected by radar, hurtled in utter silence through the sky*, it is better to write *Undetected by radar, Elizabeth hurtled silently through the sky.* Why is the second sentence better? Its streamlined order of words requires only one comma; the first version, with its helter-skelter order of words, requires two.

In *We were unaware, until last week, that the CEO, as well as the CFO, planned to resign,* the writer feels obliged to use four commas. Only one comma is necessary if we arrange the words like this: *Until last week, we were unaware that both the CEO and the CFO planned to resign.* Flow and clarity improve when you minimize the need for punctuation. Put words in straightforward order. Avoid such awkward constructions as *He, undeterred by the criticism, continued the research.* Just write *Undeterred by the criticism, he continued the research.*

3. The reader reads what the writer writes.

In other words, the reader reads what is on the page, not what is in the writer's mind. For this reason, the writer must convey his "intended" meaning and not just some meaning or other, a reasonable meaning, a near meaning, or a possible meaning. In *We will soon install the two V&G programs, DataLink and CosTrak,* how many programs are we talking about? Two or four? The sentence could be interpreted either way—but this is a sentence in a memo, not in symbolic poetry, and the reader of a memo should never need to "interpret." Note how punctuation can clarify the sense that "Datalink" and "CosTrak" are the names of the two V&G programs:

> We will soon install the two V&G programs (DataLink and CosTrak).
> We will soon install the two V&G programs—DataLink and CosTrak.
> We will soon install the two V&G programs: DataLink and CosTrak.

If the writer wishes to *suggest* that he is discussing four separate programs, he might try this:

We will soon install the two V&G programs, DataLink, and CosTrak.

But a good writer—one who will state his meaning in a way that leaves no room for "interpretation"—will reorganize the words and punctuate like this:

We will soon install DataLink, CosTrak, and the two V&G programs.

If there is one prime directive in business and technical writing, it is *Be clear*. Don't be satisfied with a "correct" sentence—insist on a *clear* one. Always review your writing and look for ambiguities. If you spot one, do whatever it takes to eliminate it. Change the words, change the order of the words, or change the punctuation. Correctness is important, but if you aren't saying what you mean, then mere correctness isn't worth very much.

4. Punctuation is never "optional."

When it comes to making decisions about punctuation, "optional" is a worm in the core of our thinking. When we think with that word, we hoax ourselves into believing that we can punctuate *if we feel like punctuating*. But punctuation is never "optional." Avoid thinking with that word; instead, begin thinking with "discretionary." It makes all the difference in the world.

Consider the often-argued-about construction called the list. *Possible side effects include loss of appetite, difficulty sleeping, violent hallucinations and dry mouth.* There is no comma after "hallucinations" because the writer believes that a comma in this position—before "and" at the end of a series—is "optional," and he doesn't *feel like* putting one in. He might feel like putting one in the next time he creates such a sentence structure, but he doesn't feel like putting one in this expression. If the writer had used discretion (a word that implies judgment, not whim), he would understand that a comma must go after "hallucinations" in that sentence. Why? Because without one, there's a *very great chance* that some readers will understand the meaning to be "violent hallucinations and violent dry mouth."

If the writer uses discretion, he understands that in *We hired two editors, four analysts and six auditors*, omitting the comma after "analysts" causes no confusion—not, at least, if the sentence stops there. In *We collected, analyzed and stored the water samples*, no comma is required after "analyzed." Why not? Because there's *very little chance* of a reader confusing "analyzed" and "stored." Judgment, judgment, judgment. A comma after "analyzed" is not incorrect, but remember Precept 2: Punctuation retards the reading. If clarity is not improved, punctuation creates needless complexity.

Here's the way to think. Ask yourself this question: *Does the reader need a comma here to prevent her from misunderstanding my meaning?* If you believe there's a reasonable chance for the reader to misunderstand, then the comma isn't optional. Put it in.

Here's something to avoid telling yourself: *My reader has common sense and can figure out what I mean.* No. It's the writer's job to "make sense" out of language; it's the reader's job to read and understand. Your sentence should be clear on the *first* reading—it should never require two or three readings and a guess disguised as an "interpretation."

5. Confusion often results when a mark plays different roles in a series.

For example, if you're using commas to separate items in a list, don't use them to surround a parenthetical expression somewhere within the list. The following sentences on the left exemplify the problem; note how clarity improves in the revisions on the right.

We brought a computer, a printer, a Hewlett-Packard "Deskwriter," and a modem.	We brought a computer, a printer (a Hewlett-Packard "Deskwriter"), and a modem.
They analyzed photographs of the Red Sea, the Strait of Hormuz, which is especially important to the region, and the Persian Gulf.	They analyzed photographs of the Red Sea, the Persian Gulf, and the Strait of Hormuz (which is especially important to the region).

6. When you proofread someone else's writing, be conservative.

If I write something like *Regardless of whether it exists; the Loch Ness Monster is necessary to our view of the world*, I would certainly hope that an editor or proofreader would change that semicolon to a comma. The semicolon is simply incorrect in that position; a comma is what is required. Such a change is "conservative" because it makes the writing *correct*. But if I write something like *The Loch Ness Monster—regardless of whether it exists—is necessary to our view of the world*, no one should tinker with the dashes. A proofreader may not like the dashes in that sentence—he may dislike dashes in general, or he may prefer commas in all such constructions, or he may believe that parentheses would do a better job in this particular case—but the punctuation is already correct, and it should not be molested.

Definitions

Ambiguity: When an expression has more than one logical (and reasonable) interpretation, that expression is ambiguous. There is no room for ambiguity in legal, business, and technical writing, but in *Backpackers report that they saw Sasquatch or Bigfoot reading the* Berkeley Gazette, we have an ambiguous remark. Is "Bigfoot" another name for "Sasquatch," or are Bigfoot and Sasquatch different creatures and the backpackers couldn't tell which one was reading the newspaper? The different meanings require different treatments; the words themselves must be slightly changed.

[If "Bigfoot" is another name for "Sasquatch."]	[If Bigfoot and Sasquatch are distinct creatures.]
Backpackers report that they saw Sasquatch ("Bigfoot") reading the *Berkeley Gazette*.	Backpackers report that they saw either Sasquatch or Bigfoot reading the *Berkeley Gazette*.

Remember Precept 1: When it comes to conveying a clear idea, the order of words is more important than punctuation will ever be. Clarify the words first.

Clause: An expression that contains a subject and a verb. There are two kinds of clauses, and here's what they look like:

Independent Clause	Dependent Clause
I see	unless I see
they discussed the contract	after they discussed the contract
the printer is malfunctioning	because the printer is malfunctioning

Dependent clause: A clause that begins with a word like *when, because, after, before, until, unless, since, although, whenever,* or *if.* The dependent clause isn't a full-fledged sentence. It's called "dependent" because, taken alone, it has no meaning; its meaning "depends" on the way it's attached to an independent clause. Here are a few more examples of dependent clauses:

whenever I try to read her writing	because the printer is malfunctioning
until we document the problem	after we receive your proposal
before he joined the company	though we have heard nothing from them

Independent clause: The basic sentence. It's called "independent" because it doesn't need anything else to be complete. Independent clauses look like this:

We interviewed 50 applicants.	The species is thriving.
These molecules are unpredictable.	Will you send the proposal?
He joined the company.	We have heard nothing from them.

List: A series of ideas. You can list nouns, verbs, adverbs, or adjectives. Here's what lists look like:

Nouns:	They have offices in New York, Chicago, Los Angeles, and Dallas.
Verbs:	We sample, test, analyze, and classify the water samples.
Adverbs:	She handled the problem quickly, thoroughly, and professionally.

Adjectives: We commend her for her quick, thorough, and professional response.

"Nonessential" versus "essential" language: In terms of punctuation, it's important to understand that these terms refer only to whether certain words or phrases are necessary in the sentence *in order for you to convey your primary intention*. For example, if I write, *Having misplaced his toupee, the CEO refused to meet with the reporter*, then I have structured the sentence in such a way that "having misplaced his toupee" is nonessential. It's nonessential because it could be omitted. If it were omitted, the sentence would read *The CEO refused to meet with the reporter*—and that's my primary meaning.

What's important to remember is that the writer—no one else—decides on the way to structure the sentence. In the original sentence, I have chosen a structure in which "having misplaced his toupee" is nonessential. Once I put those words in that order, I must punctuate accordingly. If I want the CEO's having misplaced his toupee to be essential, then I must put the words in a different order, something like *The CEO misplaced his toupee and was too embarrassed to meet with the reporter.*

Parenthetical expression: Extra stuff; a few words tossed into the middle of a sentence to clarify, explain, qualify, or amplify something. "Parenthetical" means "you could put it in parentheses." This is the big issue. *Fully one-half of the problems in punctuation result from misunderstanding (and mishandling) parenthetical words and phrases.* The thing to remember is that an expression is parenthetical if you could cut it from the sentence and the sentence (1) remains complete and (2) expresses your intended meaning. Below are some sentences containing parenthetical expressions. The "extra stuff" is in italics.

> The floppy disks, *which we ordered yesterday,* will be delivered next week.
> Her article, *"Lip-Service to Ideas,"* angered the executives.
> The board of directors—*in a move that astonished shareholders*—voted to eliminate the dividend.
> The spacecraft (*scheduled for launch on Tuesday*) is undergoing final preparation.

Phrase: In ordinary usage, a phrase is simply "two or more words." *Black cat* is a phrase. *Under the sycamore* is a phrase, as is *while observing the site.* If you're like most people, your name is a phrase. For the purposes of understanding punctuation, just keep in mind that a phrase is a collection of words that can't quite make it to the status of a clause (it lacks either a subject or a verb). Thus, *the engineer* is a phrase (it has no verb). *The engineer resisted* is a clause (it has a subject and a verb). *While observing the site* is a phrase (it has no subject), and *while we observed the site* is a clause (it now has both a subject and a verb).

The Marks

Apostrophe (')

The primary function of the apostrophe is to indicate that letters have been omitted from words. Its secondary function—and one that occurs very rarely—is to create plural forms.

Contractions

In *We're looking forward to meeting with you,* the apostrophe indicates the omission of the "a" in "are." In *She said she'd mail the proofs to us by Friday,* the apostrophe indicates the omission of "woul" in "would." Contractions are considered informal—appropriate to spoken but not to written English—and most organizations frown on their use in day-to-day business writing. Only when the occasion calls for an informal or laid-back approach should the writer use them.

Possessives

When you write *Joe's*, the apostrophe indicates the omission of "h" and "i." What you're saying with *Joe's report* is "Joe his report." What you're saying with *Ellen's suggestion* is "Ellen his suggestion."

• *When a noun (singular or plural) ends in a letter other than s, use an apostrophe and an s to form the possessive.*

| the man's decision | the men's decision | IBM's policy |
| the child's laughter | the children's laughter | the company's products |

• *When a singular noun ends in an s, simply add an apostrophe to form the plural.*

| Davis' decision | Jones' report | my boss' car |

• *When a possessive construction looks bizarre to you, find another way to show ownership.* If you think that both *Juarez' dilemma* and *Juarez's dilemma* look odd, then write about the *dilemma of Juarez.* If *Jesus' teachings* and *Jesus's teachings* both look strange to you, then phrase the idea *the teachings of Jesus.*

- *When the plural of a noun ends in* s *(as most do), add only the apostrophe to form the possessive.*

the shareholders' reaction   the companies' profits   the policies' goals

- *When the plural form of an "irregular" noun (for example,* cactus *and* criterion*) does not end in* s, *add the apostrophe and the* s *to form the plural.*

the cacti's lifespan   the criteria's focus   the phenomena's explanation

- *When there is joint ownership, only the last noun receives an apostrophe and an* s.

AT&T and MCI's proposal   Laura and Tom's honeymoon   Bill and Ted's peculiar adventure

- *In cases where there is no joint ownership, make both (or all) of the nouns possessive.*

AT&T's and MCI's proposals are nearly identical.
Laura's and Tom's ideas about housework differ radically.
Sneezy's, Dopey's, and Bashful's costumes are ready.

- *In compounds, make only the last word possessive.*

the first baseman's error   someone else's idea   the Queen of England's limousine

- *Don't use the apostrophe with possessive pronouns.*

ours (not our's) yours (not your's) theirs (not their's)
hers (not her's) its (*it's* is a
                      contraction of *it
                      is*)

- *Although no "ownership" is involved, the possessive case is conventionally used to express duration.*

one day's effort (the effort of   six months' lead time (a lead
  one day)   time of six months)
a moment's notice (the notice   nine months' revenue (the
  of one moment)   revenue of nine months)

- *Be exact when writing the names of organizations, places, and institutions.* Always follow the "authentic" form (the conventional way the name has come to be handled). *Harpers Ferry*, for example, was named for a place where a fellow named Harper once operated a ferry, and thus an English teacher would want to call it "Harper's Ferry" (using the apostrophe to indicate ownership). But the authentic form of the name (the way the name is expressed in the town charter and on all maps) lacks the apostrophe—and writers should follow that lead. It is the same with *Typesetters Union, Dramatists Guild, Johns Hopkins University*, and in every other case where names have become descriptive, rather than possessive.

The other side of this rule is that we should *use the apostrophe when the name of the organization, place, or firm conventionally uses one.* It is *Reader's Digest*, for example, not *Readers' Digest* or *Readers Digest*. Why? Simply because that's how *Reader's Digest* prefers it.

- *Use the possessive case for a noun preceding a gerund* (an *-ing* construction).

> Jack's joining the circus as a clown broke up his marriage.
> Ms. Oglethorpe's insisting that split infinitives are incorrect has made her highly popular.

Plurals

Beware. The only times the *apostrophe + s* construction is ever used to form plurals is when (1) you are making a single digit plural, (2) you are making an abbreviation that ends in a period plural, or (3) whenever the construction is absolutely necessary for clarity.

His 1's and 7's are difficult to distinguish.	the 1990s
Dot your i's and cross your t's.	F-22s
We hired three Ph.D.'s.	the ATMs
Consider the pro's and cons.	the twelve CEOs

Brackets [ ]

Brackets are used only in conjunction with quotations. When you're quoting someone and wish to comment within the quoted material, you use brackets to show that your comment isn't part of the original quotation. For example, let's say that I wish to quote an attorney who wrote something like "The takeover is clearly detrimental to the shareholders of the smaller bank." Those are her words. I have no right to change them. But if I have reason to believe that my readers will not know what the attorney meant by "the smaller bank," then I am obliged to clarify that, and I use brackets for the purpose. The result would look like this: "The takeover is clearly detrimental to the shareholders of the smaller bank [Northstar]." All the brackets do is signal the reader that an editor has added a comment.

When quoting, don't be shy about inserting words and phrases that clarify or explain what would otherwise be mysterious to the reader.

If, without context, the word "they" would be vague:	The analyst remarked, "No one knows whether they [the Federal Reserve Board] will raise interest rates."
For an audience not intimately familiar with the strange language of certain U.S. Army officers:	"Lieutenant!" Colonel Yabbis shouted. "Take that APC [armored personnel carrier] to the BARF [best available retrofit facility]! And bring me some new LPCs [leather personnel carriers, also known as "boots"] on the way back!"

Don't use brackets inside parentheses. The result may make sense logically, but it will never be easy to understand. We've all read sentences such as *The species (first discovered by Darwin [in the Galápagos] in 1830 [and believed until recently to have become extinct] on his famous voyage) is making a comeback.* This is preposterous writing. The writer must first figure out what he intends to say, and then he must say it in such a way that a fellow human can understand it on the first reading.

Colon (:)

Use a colon to (1) introduce a list, (2) alert the reader that you're setting up a summary statement, or (3) express ratio.

- *When you introduce a list, it's always best to write a complete sentence.* In other words, rather than write something like *Next year we must increase our marketing in: the Western, the Pacific Northwestern, and the Southern regions,* it is much better to write *Next year, we must increase our marketing in three regions: the West, the Pacific Northwest, and the South.* Notice how the complete sentence does a much better job of focusing the reader's expectations.

> Today we will discuss two topics: executive compensation and shareholder rights.
> She visited four countries: Portugal, Spain, France, and Italy.

- *Use a colon before a final clause, phrase, or word that explains or summarizes the preceding expression.*

> Honesty, integrity, and industriousness: These are what we value above all.
> Their "definitive" answer can be summarized in one word: *maybe*.

- *Use a colon between two independent clauses when the second independent clause explains or amplifies the first.* When you write two sentences, and the second one explains or illustrates something about the first one, the second sentence is called a "summary statement." Use a colon to introduce it. For example, if I write *I have one objection to this report. It is far too technical for its intended audience,* I have written two separate sentences. I am "correct" to punctuate that way. But because the second sentence explains what that "one objection" is, the colon is far more appropriate: It makes the relationship of the sentences instantly clear. *I have* one objection to the report: It is far too technical for its intended audience.

> The argument is suspect: It relies more on faith than on actual observation.
> She is well qualified to serve as ambassador: She is a twenty-year veteran of the mission, fluent in Russian, and exceptionally conversant in the history of the region.

- *Use a colon to express direct ratio.* Please note that direct ratio is always expressed in numerals.

a ratio of 100:1   a ratio of approximately 9:2   5:43:1

- *Do not use a colon after a verb.* It's senseless to write something like *We need to track: our indirect costs, our direct costs, and our overhead costs more diligently.* A lot of writers do this, for some reason. No colon is ever necessary after a verb. Rather than write *The agent reported: terrorist activity is imminent,* the good writer would decide how much emphasis each idea should receive, put the right words in the right order, and cast the expression in one of several ways:

A single sentence, combining the two ideas to dilute the emphasis on each one:	The agent reported that terrorist activity is imminent.
Summary statement, breaking the expression into separate independent clauses, increasing emphasis on each:	The agent reported something alarming: Terrorist activity is imminent.

| Subordinating the agent and emphasizing the terrorist activity: | According to the agent, terrorist activity is imminent. |

Comma (,)

The comma is by far the most frequently used punctuation mark; not coincidentally, it's also the most often misused. Generally speaking, people use too many commas rather than too few. (Perhaps they are panting while writing and remembering an English teacher's rule of putting in a comma each time they take a breath.)

The use of the comma is logical, systematic, and consistent. Its primary job is to separate ideas that the reader would otherwise mistakenly connect; its secondary job is to indicate the omission of a word or phrase.

- *Use a comma to separate two words or numbers that would otherwise be misunderstood.*

Of the total, overtime was the greatest single direct cost.
To his older brother, Carl remained a complete mystery.
In 1997, 618 new microbes were discovered.

- *Use a comma to separate two or more adjectives when (1) the adjectives precede the noun and (2) you could substitute "and" for the comma.*

| hot, humid day | short, sharp squawks | calm, poised, collected demeanor |

- *Don't use a comma if the adjectives are cumulative* (i.e., if you can't put "and" between them).

| atomic energy program | federal budget deficit | illegal campaign contributions |

- *Use commas to make plain that certain words, phrases, or clauses are nonessential to the meaning of the sentence.*

He has only one father:	His father, Simon, won the Nobel Prize in literature.
If there was only one foreman:	The foreman, Hank Gethers, rescued the injured worker.
If she has only one sister:	Her sister, Moira, has always been fiercely competitive.
There is only one Senate Ethics Committee:	The Senate Ethics Committee, which convened last night, voted to censure the senator.
If it was a single-pilot aircraft:	The pilot, who bailed out over Turkey, has been rescued.
If we have received only one report:	The report, received this morning, is alarming.
"Much to his astonishment" could be cut:	The botanist, much to his astonishment, found himself falling in love with a specimen.

- *Do not use commas around any words that are essential to your meaning.*

If the aircraft had two or more pilots:	The pilot who bailed out over Turkey has been rescued.
If we have received at least one other report:	The report received this morning is alarming.
if she has more than one sister:	Her sister Moira has always been fiercely competitive.

- *Commas can be used to set off contrasting elements.* (The writer could also use parentheses or dashes around these nonessential words.)

The French, not the British, designed the Concorde.
The finished document, not the draft, is what matters most.

- *Use commas to separate items in a list that ends with* and *or* or.

The participants will research, prepare, and present a technical briefing.
Complete forms 1099, 5500EZ, and 1556.
We will be represented by Alice Brown, Sam Green, or Leila Warwick.

Note: If one or more of the elements in the list requires internal commas, then commas will not suffice to separate the elements.

- *Always use a comma when you connect two independent clauses with* and, but, or, so, *or* yet. *Put the comma before the conjunction.*

We reviewed the analysis this morning, and we forwarded it to EUCOM.
She claims she wants to lose weight, yet she eats a quart of ice cream every evening.
The SEC is investigating the allegations, but the company claims it is guilty of nothing.
The work has been completed, so we should invoice the client now.
Cease the hostilities immediately, or we will authorize NATO troops to intervene.

- *Always use a comma when your sentence consists of a dependent clause followed by an independent clause. Put the comma after the dependent clause.*

>Because the diskette was damaged, we could not retrieve the data.
>After we receive the go-ahead, we will begin the final phase of the project.
>If the operation is successful, the patient should fully recover.

- *Always use a comma when your sentence opens with a phrase modifying the subject* (as in the examples below).

>Howling at the moon, the wolves seemed to epitomize the wilderness.
>While conducting the research, she discovered that Einstein's theory was flawed.
>To begin with, Lewis has always been willing to compromise.

- *When your sentence begins with a short indication of time, use discretion.* Commas are not necessary (because they do not improve clarity) in sentences like the ones below.

In 1989 the Cold War ended.   By October we expect to finish the project.

The comma does, however, aid clarity when the word immediately following the date is *uppercased,* as in the examples below.

In 1997, Lockheed Martin merged with Northrop Grumman.

By April, Smith was nearly done.

- *Conventional usage requires that you use a comma after the date when you indicate both month and day.*

On September 23, she announced her resignation.

On February 28, twenty-one protesters were jailed.

- *When you state a precise date (month, day, and year), always use a comma to separate day and year.* If the sentence continues (as in the example on the left below), put a comma after the year.

On July 6, 1997, she received the news.

The building was dedicated on January 8, 1998.

In the "European" style used by writers of military and intelligence documents, no comma is required unless it aids clarity.

> On 23 March 1997 the tanks were rolling toward Kazakhstan.
> By 1 December 1998 all agents must be proficient in the technology.
> On 17 August, Mancuso briefed the DI.
> On 9 June 1995, 364 confirmed sightings were reported.

- *Always put a comma after the clarifying devices* i.e. *and* e.g. The device *i.e.* means "that is" or "in other words"; *e.g.* means "for example." By convention, both are usually introduced in parentheses. **Note:** The usefulness of these abbreviations is limited by the fact that readers get them confused. A sensible (nonconfusable) option is to use the phrases *for example* and *that is* rather than the abbreviations.

> Several endangered species (e.g., the red wolf and the snowy owl) are being introduced into the park.
> The problems on Mir cannot be attributed to shoddy technology alone (i.e., human error has played a large role).

- *Always put a comma before* etc. When the sentence continues, punctuate after *etc.* When the sentence ends with *etc.*, the period after the abbreviation also serves to end the sentence.

> Business software (MS Office, Lotus, etc.) is becoming less and less expensive.
> Please bring the contract, the amendment, the scope of work, etc., to the meeting.
> To the meeting, please bring the contract, the amendment, the scope of work, etc.

- *Use a comma to separate elements of place names.*

> Their office is located in Potomac, Maryland, a suburb of Washington, D.C.
> He currently lives in Stuttgart, Germany.

- *Use a comma to separate the elements in people's titles when you omit prepositions.*

> She heads the Personnel Division in the Bureau of Reclamation.

Her official title is Acting Head, Personnel Division, Bureau of Reclamation.

- *Use a comma when necessary to separate digits in unrounded numbers.* Note that when you round a number, you use a decimal.

2,000   9,417   345,000   6,179,512   4,218,000
4.22 million (rounded) 4.2 million (rounded) 4 million (rounded)

- *Use a comma to indicate that you've omitted a word or words in a parallel construction.* Note the use of semicolons in this construction.

In January she loved a basketball player; in June, a baseball player; in October, a football player.
In California they have three offices; in Massachusetts, two; in Florida, one.

- *Use a comma to separate an introductory phrase from a direct quotation.*

Chairman Greenspan said, "If what I've said is clear to you, then you have not understood me."
The customer asked, "When will repairs be completed?"

- *Use a comma to set off Jr., Inc., Ltd., and so on.*

The meeting was facilitated by Harold Bubo, Jr.
Harold Bubo, Esq., lives in Vienna, Virginia.
Harry Bubo manages Greenway, Inc.

The Bubo family started Yelloway, Ltd., and merged it with Blueway, S.A., to form Greenway, Inc.

Dash (—)

Dashes emphasize things. Purely because of its lengthy shape, the dash does a better job—better than commas or parentheses—of moving ideas apart. Thus it signals the eye that something worth focusing on is about to be said. In business and technical writing, dashes are used in two ways.

• *Use dashes (instead of commas or parentheses) to surround strong parenthetical material.* Whenever you wish to put more emphasis on parenthetical stuff, you should be using dashes. If I write, *The new product, which took four years to complete, will be test-marketed in Charlotte next month*, my sentence is "correct." Commas are certainly correct there. And they would be appropriate if I wanted merely to indicate, with no particular emphasis, how many years the product took to be completed. But if I wish to stress that idea—the decision is up to me—then I should use dashes instead of commas. I should write, *The new product—which took four years to complete—will be test-marketed in Charlotte next month*. Again, this is entirely a matter of the writer's judgment.

How much emphasis should the parenthetical idea receive? Only the writer knows. She has three options—and if she remembers that the reader reads what the writer writes, she'll choose the option that best conveys her intention.

No particular emphasis: The President, reversing his position, now opposes the legislation.
Weak emphasis: The President (reversing his position) now opposes the legislation.

Strong emphasis: The President—reversing his position—now opposes the legislation.

- *Always use dashes around a parenthetical expression when that expression interrupts the flow of thought.*

> If you wish to stress the idea—the decision is up to you—then use dashes rather than commas or parentheses.
>
> We still have not heard from them—their response was due yesterday—regarding how they intend to resolve the dispute.
>
> The board of directors decided—it was a move that shocked shareholders—to eliminate the quarterly dividend.

- *The dash can be used (instead of the colon) to introduce a summary statement.*

> The property contains three families of trees—maples, oaks, and poplars.
>
> The project manager came right to the point—productivity must improve.
>
> The third use of the dash is similar to the second use of the colon—it can set up a summary statement.

Note: Keyboards don't have a single key that represents a dash. When you intend to write a dash, type two hyphens in a row. Whether you cram the dashes right beside the surrounding words—like this—or separate them from the surrounding words — like this — is a matter of fierce debate. Just be consistent.

Ellipsis Points (. . .)

Ellipsis points indicate the omission of words within quoted material. When you're quoting someone and you exclude one or more words from what that person actually said or wrote, you are obliged to use ellipsis points.

Let's say, for example, that an excited politician said, "The American public is smarter than my Aunt Millie's mule and can't be fooled for long." If you're a reporter, you may decide to cut the colorful comparison from the sentence. If you do, use the ellipsis points to indicate you've left out some words:

> The senator said, "The American public . . . can't be fooled for long."

- *When you exclude a word or words from the middle of a quoted sentence, use ellipsis points (three spaced periods).*

Leaving out "to the flag":	"I pledge allegiance . . . to the United States of America."
Leaving out "one small step for a man":	"This is . . . a giant leap for mankind."

- *When you are quoting two successive sentences and leave out the ending of the first sentence, use a period followed by three ellipsis points.*

The original quotation:	"Vampires, werewolves, and ghouls haunted her dreams when she was a child. She credits the nightmares of her childhood with fueling her adult imagination."
If you leave out the ending words of the first sentence:	"Vampires, werewolves, and ghouls haunted her. . . . She credits the nightmares of her childhood with fueling her adult imagination."

Hyphen (-)

Probably the most misunderstood of all punctuation marks, the hyphen has a single purpose—it connects ideas. It can be used to indicate a span of time, as in *He served as director from 1995–1997*. It can connect a prefix to a word (*re-sign, pro-choice, anti-inflammatory*) to form a different word. It can connect words to form a "compound noun" (the *president-elect*, a state of *self-consciousness*) or "compound verb" (She was *x-rayed*. They *soft-pedaled* the suggestion). Guidance on these issues is readily available from dictionaries and style guides.

- *Use a hyphen to avoid ambiguity.*

resign (to quit)	refund (to give money back)
re-sign (to sign again)	re-fund (to bring money in again)

- *Use a hyphen to join prefixes to capitalized nouns* (unless the combined form has acquired its own meaning).

anti-European	pre-Columbian	pro-American
transatlantic	antisemitic	subarctic

- *Use a hyphen when you spell fractions.*

one-third	a majority of two-thirds
three-quarters	a two-thirds majority

- *Use a hyphen when you give a precise numerical measurement.* Note that the numeral and the measurement (but not the noun) are hyphenated.

a 75-watt bulb	3-ton load
220-meter race	14-inch-diameter pipe

- *Use a hyphen to indicate a season that straddled two calendar years.* Note that you do not repeat the century (e.g., below, the *19* and *18* are omitted).

He averaged twenty-one points per game in the 1997-98 season.
The winter of 1883-84 was especially severe.

- *Use a hyphen to designate a continuous period of two or more years.* Note that with this construction, you do repeat the century.

The presidency of George Bush (1988-1992) was good for the domestic economy.

- *Use a hyphen to form compound nouns.*

He had a run-in with the Turkish police and is now imprisoned in Istanbul.
They marveled at the technology's cost-effectiveness.

- *Use a hyphen to indicate "suspended compounds"* (where the important element is omitted in all but the last term).

The lumber is available in 8-, 16-, and 32-foot lengths.
The proposal indicates both pre- and post-completion costs.

- *Use a hyphen to clarify "improvised usage" when forming compound adjectives.* This is what causes the most confusion, so we'll spend some time discussing it.

First of all, it's important to understand that the hyphen gives you infinite flexibility in the order of words. That's significant because English (unlike many other languages) depends on the order of words for meaning. *The cat ate the rat* and *The rat ate the cat* consist of the same words, but the meanings are very different.

Second, please understand that emphasis—how much attention a word receives—depends on where that word is in a sentence. The last word in a sentence is always emphatic. For example, *We have received the report from the fourth quarter* emphasizes the quarter, but *We have received the fourth-quarter report* emphasizes the report. Both are fine, but what do you wish to emphasize—the quarter, or the report? You could write about an *adjustment to the cost of living* or about a *cost-of-living adjustment*. Both are fine, but what do you want to emphasize—"living," or "adjustment"? The reader reads whatever you write, so it's essential that you emphasize the right idea.

Let's suppose you're writing about a certain contract. You might write *the contract that lasts for six months* or *the six-month contract*. Why is "six-month" hyphenated? Here's why. In *the contract that lasts for six months*, "months" is a noun and "six" is an adjective. When (for the sake of emphasis) you change the order of words to *the six-month contract*, "month" isn't functioning as a noun anymore. Instead, it's functioning as an adjective. But it isn't the sort of adjective that makes sense by itself; in other words, the contract isn't both a "month" contract *and* a "six" contract. "Six-month" is a unit, behaving as a single adjective, and so you hyphenate.

Contrast *Her father bought her a little-used car* and *Her father bought her a little, used car*. In the first instance, the hyphen lets us know that the car (whatever its size) hadn't been driven very much. In the second instance, the comma lets us know that the car was both a small car *and* a used car.

To answer the question *Should I hyphenate?*, just ask yourself whether you could put the word "and" between adjectives. A *hot and humid day* becomes a *hot, humid day* because the day is both "hot" *and* "humid." But a *nation that speaks English* becomes an *English-speaking nation* because the nation isn't both a "speaking" nation *and* an "English" nation.

a report of 50 pages	a 50-page report
taxpayers who earn a high income	high-income taxpayers
a son who is eighteen years old	an eighteen-year-old son
expenses paid out of your own pocket	your out-of-pocket expenses
a race of 100 meters	a 100-meter dash
a plan that allows you to pay as you go	a pay-as-you-go plan

- *When a phrase is familiar and the hyphen does not aid clarity, it can be omitted.*

federal budget deficit	ground attack aircraft
Social Security legislation	human rights violations

- *Don't hyphenate* two-word compounds *when the first word is an adverb ending in* -ly.

quickly reached verdict	unusually vigorous response

- *Don't hyphenate compounds when the first word is comparative or superlative.*

most favored nation	more advantageous solution
best kept secret	less developed countries

- *Don't hyphenate foreign phases used as adjectives.*

pro forma ceremony	ad hoc committee

- Finally, always consult a current dictionary or style guide to determine whether a particular compound is spelled as two words, hyphenated, or spelled as one word.

Parentheses ( )

- *Use parentheses to introduce acronyms and abbreviations (including abbreviations of measurement).*

> He is being transferred to the European Command (EUCOM) next month.
> The Organization of Petroleum Exporting Countries (OPEC) cannot agree on a quota.
> We will introduce an Employee Stock Ownership Plan (ESOP) next year.
> Tachometers measure revolutions per minute (rpm).
> The maximum safe level of radon is 4 picocuries per liter of air (4 pc/l).

- *Use parentheses to introduce formal and technical symbols.*

> She decided to buy 500 shares of Eli Lilly (LLY).
> The "percent" symbol (%) must be confined to tables and graphs.

- *Use parentheses to enclose numbers in a series.*

> After only one hour with him, she believed that (1) the Loch Ness Monster existed, (2) Elvis was alive and living in Edinburgh, and (3) aliens preferred haggis to any other Scottish food.

- *Use parentheses to set off a word, phrase, or clause that you insert merely by way of clarifying comment or explanation.* Such comments (called "asides") will then be understood to have only minor importance. Please note the placement of the periods in the third and fourth example below.

> Only one complainant (Jones) is willing to settle before trial.
> Herpetology (the study of reptiles) is fascinating.
> The Pentagon is headquarters for the Department of Defense (previously called the War Department).
> The audit discovered three discrepancies. (All have since been corrected.)

- *Use parentheses to introduce* i.e. *and* e.g.

> Illuminated manuscripts (e.g., *The Book of Kells*) are magnificent works of art.
> All exempt employees (i.e., those who receive an annual salary) are expected to take a polygraph test.

- *Use parentheses to enclose cross-references.*

> Income distribution remains skewed (see Table 2).
> While making a comeback in some areas, the species remains endangered (see Appendix C).

Parentheses With Other Punctuation

- *When a sentence begins in parentheses, put the period (or question mark or exclamation point) inside parentheses.*

The analysis indicates a massive shift in consumers' buying habits. (They are beginning to put off buying big-ticket items.)

Artificial intelligence remains artificial. (Computers still cannot reason.)

- *When the expression inside parentheses ends a longer sentence, put the period outside parentheses.*

Send your resume to Ms. Sharon Oliver (Chairperson, Selection Committee).

The species now proliferates in Maryland waters (scientists disagree about its origin).

- *Follow the standards when using parentheses along with commas, colons, dashes, and semicolons.* Below are a few examples.

Commas before parentheses because parentheses enumerate a list:	After only one hour with him, she believed that (1) the Loch Ness Monster existed, (2) Elvis was alive and living in Edinburgh, and (3) aliens preferred haggis.
Comma after parentheses because the parentheses describe an item in a list:	He visited Oxford (Pennsylvania), Cambridge (Maryland), and Paris (Virginia).
Comma after parentheses because the parentheses end a dependent clause:	Since we last heard from her (three weeks ago), she has made amazing progress.
A semicolon after parentheses because another independent clause follows:	The Redskins are 3-1 (their best start in five years); their schedule is tougher from now on.

Period (.)

Everyone agrees that the period ends a declarative sentence. That's its only job.

While I doubt there's been any research on this issue, I'll bet that in a given 1,000-word document, good writers use more periods than bad writers do. That's because they'll write more (shorter) sentences. *Always keep in mind that to isolate is to emphasize.* The period ends the sentence, yes, but it also segregates the idea and isolates it. Thus, it is perfectly correct to write *The committee has voted to begin impeachment proceedings against Senator Gonzofrew; the senator vehemently denies any abuse of power.* But if the writer wished to emphasize each idea, he would put each into a separate sentence. *The committee has voted to begin impeachment proceedings against Senator Gonzofrew. The senator vehemently denies any abuse of power.* Short sentences punch the meaning home. Longer sentences, containing numerous ideas, dilute emphasis on any thought.

Question Mark (?)

The question mark ends the interrogative sentence. *When does the meeting begin? When the writer writes "bimonthly," what does he mean?*

A sentence must end with a question mark when any element within it asks a direct question. If you write *We can assume that revenue will increase*, you have written a declarative sentence. You end it with a period. But consider *We can assume, can't we, that revenue will increase?* That little *can't we*, which is called an "interjection" because the writer just tosses it in, asks a direct question. That tiny question contaminates the entire expression, and the sentence has to end with a question mark.

Writers often make the mistake of putting question marks at the end of sentences that aren't truly questions. *Should we proceed?* is a question. *I wonder whether we should proceed* is a statement. Do not write *I wonder whether we should proceed?*

Quotation Marks (" ")

- *Use quotation marks to indicate that someone else (not you) either said or wrote the exact words.*

> According to the mission specialist, the Mars landing is a "spectacular scientific achievement."
> In his report, Jones states that "demographic shifts are in our favor."
> When asked why he did not take the shorter route, the truck driver replied, "I'm taking this route because this is the route I always take. I've taken this route all my life, and I'm not changing it!"

- *Use quotation marks to indicate that a particular word or phrase is ironic.*

> the 1986 Tax "Simplification" Act (it complicated everyone's taxes)
> "safe" havens in Bosnia (they were in fact very dangerous places to be)

- *Use quotation marks to introduce an unfamiliar or technical term.*

> The robot's "end effectors" (i.e., hands) are almost as dexterous as a human's.
> When the rate of increase slows, economists call the phenomenon "negative growth."

- *Use quotation marks to indicate that you're talking about an expression, as opposed to meaning anything with the expression.*

> Barnes uses the word "proactive" far too often.
> BARF is derived from the phrase "best available retrofit facility."

- *Use quotation marks to set off the titles of poems and songs, and to set off a discrete section of a larger document.*

> In college she had to memorize Frost's poem "Stopping by Woods on a Snowy Evening."
> Chapter 3, "The Double Helix," is the most important chapter of her book, *Theory of Genetics*.
> In the December 4 issue of *Time*, there is a fascinating article entitled "Life in the Fast Lane."
> "On the Street Where You Live" is her favorite song from *West Side Story*.

- *Use "single" quotation marks only when you must quote something within a quotation.* (The apostrophe serves this purpose.)

> According to the memo, "Documents classified as 'Secret' or higher may not be reproduced except in secure areas."
> In the preface, the author writes, "The danger of such phrases as 'functional illiteracy' is that they demand interpretation."

Quotation Marks With Other Punctuation

- *The period always goes inside quotation marks.* This is simply the convention in America. It is an inviolate rule; there are no exceptions.

According to the affidavit, "Suggestive remarks were made on several occasions."
The engineer characterized the construction as "flimsy."
"I think," she said mysteriously, "that you're in for a pleasant surprise."

• *The comma always goes inside quotation marks.* This is (like the placement of the period) the convention in American usage. It is a rule. There are no exceptions.

They call it a "wooden interdental stimulator," but it's really just a toothpick.
"The design is superb," the customer said.
"The design is superb," the customer said, "but I wish the house weren't so expensive."

• *The colon, dash, and semicolon always go outside quotation marks.* This is not a rule, per se, but it may as well be one. Here's why. Chances are zero that you will ever choose to quote someone and end the quotation where the person used (for example) a colon. That makes no sense at all. But you could easily decide to use the quotation as a lead-in to a list or summary statement, and in that case, using the colon would be your decision (and certainly not part of the original quotation). Precisely the same logic holds for the dash and for the semicolon.

"A foolish consistency is the hobgoblin of little minds": Thus did Emerson summarize his disgust with narrow-minded thinking.
According to Shakespeare, "Hell hath no fury like a woman scorned"; Shakespeare never had to deal with

outraged alligators, and he might have thought differently if he had.

"This species," the biologist said, "devours itself in captivity"—a phenomenon that animal psychologists term "depressive autocannibalism."

- *The question mark goes inside quotation marks only (and always) when the quoted material is a question* (as in the first two examples below). When the overall sentence is a question, but the quoted material is simply a declarative statement, then the question mark goes outside the quotation marks (as in the last example below).

A statement about a question:	The auditor asked point-blank, "Exactly when will we receive the finished report?"
A question about a question:	Did the client ask, "Will you itemize the charges on the invoice?"
A question about a statement:	Do the instructions read, "Attach the red wire to the positive and the black wire to the negative"?

- *Like the question mark, the exclamation point goes inside quotation marks only (and always) when the quoted material is exclamatory* (as in the first two examples below). When the overall sentence is exclamatory, but the quoted material is simply a declarative statement, place the exclamation point outside quotation marks (as in the last example).

A statement about an exclamation:	The excited politician cried, "I'll vote any which way they want me to!"
An exclamation about an exclamation:	I hate it when I hear commercials blaring, "Breakfast is the most important meal of the day!"

An exclamation about a statement:	We must respond instantly to their remark, "Ours is the superior product"!

Note: When you end a sentence with a quotation, use only one "ending indicator" (a period, a question mark, or an exclamation point). Never use two marks.

- *When you precede the quotation with an attribution (i.e., who said or wrote the words) and you are quoting an entire sentence, put a comma after the attribution, as follows.*

> Davis muttered, "Why am I always the last one to know?"
> The report concludes, "Consolidation will certainly continue in the banking industry."

- *When you give the attribution at the end of the quotation, punctuate with a comma, question mark, or exclamation point, as appropriate.*

> "We have every reason to be optimistic," the attorney insisted.
> "I want my pipe and my slippers!" her grandfather exclaimed.
> "Can we expect increased earnings in the fourth quarter?" the CEO asked.

- *When you interrupt a quotation with an attribution, punctuate with commas, as follows.* Note that two sets of quotation marks are used.

> "My point," he said, "is that we could be much more productive."

"Why is it," the author asks, "that physics leads to religion?"

- *When you're quoting only a fragment, and not the entire sentence, no comma is required before the quotation.*

According to the quarterly report, a dividend increase "will certainly occur this year."
She called the lawsuit "ridiculous and frivolous."

- *Use quotation marks after such words as* named, entitled, termed, signed, *and so forth.* Note that no comma precedes the quotation.

The accompanying card was signed "Your One and Only."
He was named "Most Likely to Succeed" by his classmates.
The report entitled "From Technology to Metatechnology" offers a fascinating perspective.

Semicolon (;)

Even the name of this thing is trouble. It should be called a "supercomma" or a "semiperiod" (because its practical effect is to bring things to a near-stop). But someone named it semi*colon*, and the name stuck, and there's not much we can do about it. In business writing, this misunderstood mark can be used in four ways.

- *A semicolon may be used to connect independent clauses when there is no conjunction.* Generally speaking, the semicolon works best when the two independent clauses are parallel in structure, as in the examples below.

> CMX employs 90,000 people; AFG employs 146,000.
> This year's RFP generated 134 proposals; last year's generated 120; two years ago, it generated only 111.

- *A semicolon may be used to connect two independent clauses when the second independent clause is introduced by a transitional phrase.*

> The new procedure will save time and money; more to the point, it will increase safety.
> A new CEO will be hired next year; in the interim, Smith will serve as chief executive.
> The chain of custody was unclear; as a result, the judge threw out the evidence.

- *A semicolon may be used to connect two independent clauses when the second independent clause is introduced by what English teachers call a "conjunctive adverb."*

> We cannot publish your novel at this time; nevertheless, we encourage you to keep writing.
> The method must be repeatable; otherwise, the results will be considered invalid.
> Our competitors are gaining market share; furthermore, they are expanding overseas.

- *A semicolon may be used to separate items in a list when one or more of those items contains parenthetical information (and hence has to have a comma in it).*

> Next year we plan to revise the vacation policy; the maternity leave policy, which has not been updated since 1978; and the early retirement policy.

Note: The construction above, while "correct," leaves much to be desired in terms of readability. When the items in your list require semicolons, it is much simpler to format the list vertically. When you do so, neither commas nor semicolons are required for the separation of the items. Note also that there is no period at the end of the vertical list. The format indicates, at a glance, how the items are separated and when the list ends.

> Next year we plan to revise three polices:
> - Vacation
> - Maternity leave (which has not been updated since 1978)
> - Early retirement

Slash (/)

The best advice regarding the slash is to use it as sparingly as possible. Everyone has encountered the confusion that this mark causes when used sloppily, as in the phrase *air/ground communications*. Some readers will interpret this construction to mean a reciprocal relationship (that communication can be initiated either from the aircraft or from the ground). What the writer means is *air-to-ground* only. The hyphens reveal what he means; the slash conceals it.

- *Use the slash to indicate "per" in highly technical abbreviations.*

pc/l (picocuries per liter of air)

m^3/sec (cubic meters per second)

Practical Punctuation 149

> • *Use the slash to indicate a twelve-month period overlapping two calendar years.*

fiscal year 1998/99   academic year 1972/73

> • *Use the slash in the construction "and/or" only after you have considered the alternatives.* Most of the time, you mean only "and"; sometimes you mean "or." Very rarely do you mean both. *Bring your passport and/or driver's license to the interview* exemplifies the problem. If both documents are required, then the right word is "and." If only one document is required, then the right word is "or."

In the example below, arbitration may be chosen by either party alone, or by both. Apparently both parties do not have to agree.

> The union and/or company may choose arbitration.

But if both parties do not have to agree, doesn't it make better sense to use "or"?

> Either the union or company may choose arbitration.

In the example below, however, the writer is expressing uncertainty. Trees are dying on the mountainside, and scientists are unsure why.

> The deforestation is attributed to microscopic parasites and/or chemical pollution.

Some say that the trees are dying because of man-made pollution; others say that the problem is not pollution, but a tiny parasite. And others insist that both the parasite and the pollution are responsible. Here's a case where *it could be both, or it could be either one.* The important issue here—the key—is that *we don't know yet.*

Either (or both) could have caused the crash. We don't know yet:	The crash was caused by mechanical failure and/or pilot error.
Either (or both) could be the reason for the jump in earnings. We don't know yet:	The jump in earnings results from increased advertising and/or increased prices.

Relationships Between Clauses

The order of words—the sentence structure—dictates punctuation. Here are the common sentence structures and the appropriate ways to punctuate them.

S V and V   One subject and two verbs.

> We arrived at the site and inspected the damage.
> The CEO glanced at the executive summary and howled in dismay.
> The new text will simplify and clarify our policy.
> The animal has escaped and is loose somewhere in the lab.
> The agency monitors and regulates toxic waste sites.

Note that there is *no punctuation* when (1) one subject does two things and (2) nothing in the sentence is parenthetical.

S and S V   Two subjects and one verb.

> Sticks and stones may break your bones.
> The CEO and the EVP agree that the stock should be split.

Practical Punctuation

> Your proposal and supporting documents are due on the tenth.
> Men and women have different biological imperatives.
> The CIA and the FBI have repeatedly argued about jurisdiction in this case.

Note that there is *no punctuation* when (1) two subjects take the same verb and (2) nothing is parenthetical.

IC IC   Two independent clauses without any conjunction.

There are five different ways to punctuate between two independent clauses when we do not connect them with words. We can use a period, a semicolon, a colon, a dash, or parentheses. Each mark suggests a different relationship between the clauses.

- *Use a period when each idea is equally important and you wish each idea to receive maximum weight.*

> We received your proposal yesterday. It will be evaluated next week.
> Fannie Mae's stock rose yesterday. Freddie Mac's stock fell.

- *Use a semicolon between independent clauses when (1) the structures are parallel and (2) you wish to dilute the emphasis of each idea.*

> Fannie Mae's stock rose yesterday; Freddie Mac's stock fell.

The CFO promptly resigned; the CEO vowed to fight the takeover.

• *Use a colon when the second independent clause amplifies or explains the first.* This construction, known as a "summary statement," is a particularly powerful aid to coherence.

Their argument contained a logical flaw: Subsequence does not imply consequence.
The dictator learned something important: Brutality does not work.

• *Use a dash, instead of a colon, when (1) the second independent clause amplifies the first and (2) you wish to suggest that the outcome is fairly dramatic.*

The experiment suggests something incredible—the speed of light can be surpassed.
The project manager came right to the point—the overruns must stop.

• *Use parentheses around the second independent clause when you wish to indicate that the second one is less important than the first.*

We received your proposal yesterday. (It will be evaluated next week.)
We received your proposal yesterday (it will be evaluated next week).

Note: In these examples the period goes inside parentheses when the sentence begins in parentheses. The period goes outside parentheses when both of the independent clauses are contained in a single-sentence structure. Either construction is correct. The first example maximizes the weight of *We received your proposal yesterday*. The second example dilutes emphasis on that idea because both independent clauses are contained in a single-sentence structure.

Also note: *Do not use a comma between two independent clauses when there is no conjunction.* This is a very common error, and what results is called a "comma splice" or a "run-on sentence." Below are some examples with suggested correct revisions. *Remember that you can use a period, a semicolon, a colon, a dash, or parentheses.* The precise mark you use depends on how you want the clauses to relate.

Wrong: The new policy is certain to create confusion, it is unclearly written.
Correct: The new policy is certain to create confusion: It is unclearly written.
Wrong: We are responsible for the design, they are responsible for the execution.
Correct: We are responsible for the design; they are responsible for the execution.
Wrong: The vampire stood in the firelight, its fangs gleamed.
Correct: The vampire stood in the firelight. Its fangs gleamed.

IC, and IC Two independent clauses connected by a short conjunction.

The familiar "compound sentence" consists of two or more independent clauses with a short (one-syllable) conjunction between them. When you connect independent clauses with *and, but, or, so,* or *yet,* place a comma immediately before the conjunction.

> The audit team found several discrepancies, and the bank has agreed to rectify them.
> The audit team found several discrepancies, but the bank refuses to rectify them.

The consultant broke his leg, so he missed the meeting.
You can continue using this policy, or you can create a more effective one.
The witness has been granted immunity, yet she refuses to testify.
They lost the account, for they did not listen to the customer. (Archaic)
They lost the account because they did not listen to the customer. (Contemporary)

A comma always goes before those five short conjunctions. No other mark ever does. The last example, which connects the sentences with "because," requires no comma.

IC; however, IC   Two independent clauses connected by a longer conjunction.

We do not use a comma before connecting words and phrases that are longer than one syllable. A comma always goes *after* these expressions, but what you put in front of them depends on precisely what you intend to convey. Use a period, a dash, a semicolon, or parentheses.

Consider the sentence *The team thoroughly investigated the site, but they could find no evidence of contamination.* That construction is the familiar compound sentence, where two independent clauses are connected with "but." The comma is the right mark there. If the writer uses "however" instead of "but," there are four (and only four) ways to punctuate:

If both ideas are equally important and should have maximum weight, use a period to create separate sentences:	The team thoroughly investigated the site. However, they could find no evidence of contamination.
If both ideas are equally important, but	The team thoroughly investigated the

Practical Punctuation

you wish to dilute emphasis on each one, use a semicolon.	site; however, they could find no evidence of contamination.
If you wish to suggest that the second independent clause is an especially significant outcome, use a dash:	The team thoroughly investigated the site—however, they could find no evidence of contamination.
If you wish to suggest that the second independent clause is less important than the first one, use parentheses:	The team thoroughly investigated the site (however, they could find no evidence of contamination).

Note that the comma always goes after the longer conjunction, but never before it. In the examples above, we've used "however" instead of "but." Precisely the same pattern holds when the writer uses "otherwise" instead of "or," when he uses "therefore" instead of "so," when he uses "nevertheless" instead of "yet," or when he uses "furthermore" or "moreover" instead of "and."

The same pattern holds for phrases that are used to connect sentences. If you think about it, the phrases *as a result* and *as a consequence* mean the same thing as "so" or "therefore." But these phrases are not one-syllable conjunctions, and they require the same treatment as "therefore."

Example: Scientists have expressed concern about the safety of the Pocomoke; as a result, the Maryland Department of Natural Resources has banned all recreational activities in the river.

DC, IC A dependent clause followed by an independent clause.

After we make our selection, we will notify you.

If you have any questions, please contact Ms. O'Rourke.

Unless we hear otherwise, we will assume that the meeting will occur.

Because they wished to take advantage of inexpensive labor, they moved their manufacturing facilities to Mexico.

Note that you put a comma immediately after the dependent clause. A comma always goes there; nothing else ever does.

IC DC An independent clause followed by a dependent clause.

> We will notify you after we make our selection.
> Please contact Ms. O'Rourke if you have any questions.
> Pay strict attention to consistency when you edit your report.
> The plaintiff maintains that she wasn't informed until the deadline had passed.

No punctuation goes anywhere in these sentences (just the opposite of DC, IC).

IC, IC, and IC A list of three or more independent clauses.

> GTA did the research, BGG wrote the report, and XVT implemented the process.
> DDI adopted the policy three years ago, FVI adopted it last year, and next month EIF will adopt it as well.

Note: The use of semicolons would be inappropriate here because commas suffice to separate the ideas. For the same reason that we swat a fly with a flyswatter (and not drop a hydrogen bomb on it), we use minimal force when punctuating. Remember too that by putting all of these independent clauses into one sentence structure, the writer is heavily diluting the emphasis on each. Emphasis would be rescued if the writer used periods and made each independent clause into a separate sentence.

IC [however, furthermore, therefore, etc.] IC.

If you use longer conjunctions between sentences, always put a comma after the conjunction. One of four marks goes in front of it—the period, the semicolon, the dash, or the beginning of parentheses (depending on your emphasis). Below we use "however" instead of "but." This is how you handle it.

IC. However, IC. The reasoning you use here is precisely the same as the
IC; however, IC. reasoning explained in the "IC IC" section above.
IC—however, IC.
IC (however, IC).
IC. (However, IC.)

Quick Reading	Slow Reading
IC, and IC.	IC. Moreover, IC.
	IC—in addition, IC.
	IC; furthermore, IC.
IC, but IC.	IC (however, IC).
IC, so IC.	IC. Therefore, IC.
	IC—as a result, IC.
	IC; consequently, IC.
IC, or IC.	IC; otherwise, IC.
IC, yet IC.	IC (still, IC).
	IC. Nevertheless, IC.

Punctuation at a Glance

DC, IC	Use a comma (never any other mark) to separate DC from IC.
IC DC	If the IC comes first, don't punctuate.
IC. IC.	Both sentences are equal in weight. Both ideas have maximum weight.
IC: IC.	Second sentence explains the first.
IC; IC.	Sentence structures are parallel; they are equal in weight and importance.
IC—IC.	Second sentence is dramatic outcome of first.
IC (IC).	Second sentence paraphrases the first.
IC. (IC.)	Second sentence less important than the first.
IC, and IC. IC, but IC. IC, or IC. IC, yet IC. IC, so IC.	If you use these one-syllable conjunctions to connect two independent clauses, always insert a comma.

Part Four
Electronic Writing

Electronic Mail

A long time ago, before civilization really got going, there was a fellow named Mudrok. One day Mudrok was standing on a hillside, looking at the sky and drooling (as was his habit). (Why Mudrok habitually did these things will be clarified in a moment.) Suddenly, he was struck by an amazing idea. It was an idea so new, so brilliant, so utterly different that no one had ever had one like it before. It was an idea that would completely revolutionize life in Mudrok's village—simplify it, streamline it, enhance it, and in general make it much better than it ever had been. Unfortunately, no one knows what Mudrok's idea was. When he mentioned it to the townspeople, all they could do was laugh. Mudrok, you see, was the village idiot. All the non-idiots, reasoning in a circular way, believed that anything a village idiot said would be, by definition, idiotic. They slapped their thighs, they guffawed, they laughed until they wept. And so Mudrok's wonderful idea was lost forever, simply because Mudrok was the one who had it.

Mudrok and electronic mail have a lot in common. Many people regard email as the village idiot of business correspondence, capable of little more than capering foolishness. That's unfortunate because email can be a very powerful communications tool if it's used appropriately. And one thing is certain: The medium is here to stay, and business writers must learn how to use it well.

Just as it was illogical for Mudrok's companions to disregard his idea merely because it was his, it is illogical to believe that ideas conveyed through email cannot be taken seriously. Being serious—being clear—is up to the writer. Once we accept this fact, then complaints about email as a medium are seen in their true light, as excuses for weak or hasty writing.

Electronic Mail at Home

Good writing is writing that suits the occasion. When you're using your home computer, on your own time, you are perfectly free to write whatever you like, in any style you like. If you're at home, sending a message to your brother in Stuttgart, it makes no sense to pretend you don't know him and to adopt a rigorously formal approach. When I send email to my brother, the writing is relaxed, personal, relatively informal; many of the "rules" of English go out the window. (This is because I have a relatively relaxed brother. If my brother were a stickler in matters of punctuation and grammar, and I wanted him to take me seriously, I would have to observe his preferences.)

The style and tone of communication mirror the occasion and relationship, as they should. If the subject is frivolous, I can be creative with my spelling, clown around with words, write long and ramshackle sentences, muse at length about trivia, and digress for the fun of it. I can do these things when I send email to my brother because I'm writing the frivolous email for his entertainment and amusement. He doesn't have to read it if he doesn't want to. My email doesn't occupy his at-work time, and he doesn't have to make important decisions, change his behavior, or put a meeting on his calendar because of it. I'm not attempting to sell him anything, and because he knows I can write reasonably well when I want to, my reputation is not at risk.

When I send email to the Pentagon, confirming a contract, I'm a lot more careful with every aspect of good writing.

Electronic Mail in the Workplace

As is true of all writing, the style and tone of electronic mail should be appropriate to the occasion and to your relationship with your readers. And these things vary, even at work. A quick announcement that the executive vice president's new baby is a brawling "eight-pounder" named Heather requires a treatment different from the announcement that a project is being terminated and layoffs are imminent. The first requires a lighthearted approach; the second requires straightforwardness and compassion. (Some individuals actually do use email (at work) for messages such as baby announcements, which might be more appropriately conveyed in other ways. The overuse of email for such personal announcements (i.e., nonbusiness issues) is probably the chief reason why so many people regard email as a plaything.)

This brief section of *Write for Results* is concerned only with electronic correspondence in the workplace. Before we can get started, we have to assume that a number of things are true.

First, we assume that the writer has something to say, and that this subject (whatever it may be) is important or useful to one or more readers.

Second, we assume that the writer has a relatively serious subject and wishes his ideas to be taken seriously.

Third, we assume that the writer is courteous. This

means not only that he takes his readers' feelings into account, but respects their time as well.

Fourth, we assume that the writer is conscientious. This means, in essence, that he works hard to make his ideas clear on first reading. In other words, he works hard so that the reader won't have to.

Finally, we assume that for some reason the writer can't simply use the telephone and leave a message in voice mail. In terms of sheer efficiency, the only times when email is preferable to voice mail are when (1) the writer has a multiple audience and doesn't want to leave the same message on a number of answering machines, (2) the writer is using email to send a lengthy document as an attachment, or (3) the writer's message is extremely detailed (e.g., an itinerary, directions to a site, etc.) and the recipient would have to replay the message to capture all of the important facts.

The chief complaints about email involve writers' ignoring these five issues. Everywhere I go, when I ask people about their experience with email, I hear the same complaints.

- The majority of the email people receive at work is frivolous, useless, or even downright silly.
- The writer sends email to a massive number of people when only a few truly need the information.
- The writer sends CCs to individuals who are neither involved in nor interested in the issue.
- The writer tries to be humorous but forgets that tone of voice, facial expression, and gesture are all just as important as words in making a statement funny. The result is that attempts at humor come across as sarcasm, which can easily hurt and offend. Equally subversive are the obnoxious little "happy faces" that

insecure humorists dutifully sprinkle onto the page, lest we misunderstand their intent. (We have all been plagued by them. The look like this: :-). There should be a bounty on them in business writing.)
- The writer does not pay enough attention to the ordinary mechanics of language. Spelling, punctuation, grammar, word choice, word order—all are treated with the utmost indifference. A sloppy presentation not only obstructs reading and diminishes the seriousness of the issue but it also reflects badly on the writer.
- The writer does not bother with the essentials of formatting and fails to supply the "reader direction" (e.g., headings, subheadings, vertical lists) that is so common, and helpful, in memos and reports.
- The Subject line is usually vague, and the writer does not quickly come to the point. The reader is forced to hunt for the main idea.

Writing Effectively in Electronic Mail

Email imposes a number of constraints on writers. Here are some tips on ways to write effectively within those constraints.

1. Take extra care with the Subject line.

In the Subject line, strive to be as precise and as accurate as you can. In most email applications, only the first twenty characters or so (of Subject lines) can fit onto the screen, and from glancing at these few characters readers decide whether the message is (1) relevant to them and (2) worth reading.

Example

Hypothetically, the point of the following email is that the building will be closing at noon this Friday, and will remain closed until 6 A.M. next Monday, because representatives of OSHA will be visiting to install radon-monitoring devices. The writer wants his readers to know that they must leave the building at noon. In this case, which of the two Subject lines below is more accurate?

```
         To:  All employees (mass@company.org)
       From:  Henry Gnober (gnoberh@company.org)
    Subject:  Radon test
         CC:
        BCC:
Attachments:
```

```
         To:  All employees (mass@company.org)
       From:  Henry Gnober (gnoberh@company.org)
    Subject:  Early dismissal on Friday
         CC:
        BCC:
Attachments:
```

The first Subject line, "Radon test," may interest some employees, but the second one, "Early dismissal on Friday," will interest everyone. (And help to ensure that the document is read.) Just as importantly, given the main point of the document, "Early dismissal on Friday" is far more accurate and precise than "Radon test." Always try to be as precise as possible in the Subject line.

2. Come to the point.

If you could say one sentence to your reader, what sentence would you say?

That should be the first question you answer, and you should know the answer before you try to write. That sentence will be the reason you're writing—the point you're trying to make—and usually it's best to reveal it right away. If you withhold the point, attempting to supply background information, most readers ignore your intention and scan for the main idea. The only times when coming to the point is inappropriate are when (1) you need to persuade readers to do something or (2) your news is harmful or upsetting. And in those cases, email is probably not the proper medium for the message.

Example

Continuing with our previous scenario, let's examine two different ways to organize the ideas.

To:	All employees (mass@company.org)
From:	Henry Gnober (gnoberh@company.org)
Subject:	Early dismissal on Friday
CC:	
BCC:	
Attachments:	

As you know, the U.S. Environmental Protection Agency (EPA) tested this facility for radon one month ago. EPA's test indicated that the level of radon in this building is well within federal safety guidelines. It has since come to my attention, however, that EPA's manner of testing is considered unreliable by many experts. Therefore, we are asking the Occupational Safety and Health Administration (OSHA) to visit and conduct another test. OSHA's test is generally considered to be far more reliable than EPA's.

Radon is an invisible gas emitted by rocks and soil. It is a known cancer-causing agent. The health and safety of our employees are important to us, and if OSHA's test reveals an unacceptable level of radon in the building, we will take appropriate steps to remedy the situation. We would, for example, reglaze the interior walls of the underground garage and the first floor; we would also install a central air-purifying system.

The installation of the radon-monitoring devices will begin at noon this Friday and will continue through the weekend. OSHA recommends that the building be closed for this work. All employees are asked to leave the building at noon on the 13th and return to work on Monday the 16th at their regular time.

Rest assured that we will continue to monitor the radon level.

        To: All employees (mass@company.org)
     From: Henry Gnober (gnoberh@company.org)
  Subject: Early dismissal on Friday
        CC:
      BCC:
Attachments:

All employees are asked to leave the building at noon this Friday. Representatives of OSHA will be installing radon-monitoring devices over the weekend, and the building will be closed until 6 a.m. Monday, February 16. Normal business hours will resume on that day.

We have invited OSHA to test for radon merely as a precaution. EPA's recent test of our facility indicated a safe level of radon in the building; OSHA's test, however, is generally considered to be more reliable than EPA's, and we will take no chances where employees' health is concerned.

OSHA's test requires 30 days to complete. The results will be distributed as soon as we receive them.

Which of those versions would you rather read? If you're like most readers in the workplace (that is, busy), you strongly prefer the second. The writer comes straight to the point, which (1) prevents you from having to spend time hunting for the main idea and (2) maximizes the chance that you will get the point before your telephone rings and you are called away on an emergency.

    The writer of the first version has committed a number of errors—not of writing, per se, but of assumption. He has forgotten, for example, that in the business environment, people do not read for pleasure. (They will scan his extensive background information until they see his point, and then they may or may not go back and read the background material.) He has also forgotten that he does not need to justify, certainly not at such length, OSHA's visit. And one explanatory sentence begets another, and the second begets another, and so on, all the while needlessly delaying the point.

If you are unused to being direct—to revealing the main sentence early—then coming to the point may seem awkward to you at first. It may strike you as being abrupt, curt, or even rude. If it does, then please remember that you preferred the second version above. You preferred it; so will your readers.

Practice coming to the point. In time it will become habitual, and your readers will applaud you for it.

3. Isolate a sentence to emphasize it.

In email, this is the only way to make certain that a given sentence will stand out. Surround it with space; let it appear as a paragraph.

Even if your email application enables you to boldface or italicize text on *your* screen, there's no guarantee that such graphics will show up on the recipient's screen. Strange things happen on the Internet (and even within many Local Area Networks, or LANs). More often than not, formatting changes get filtered out. Text reverts to the "default" setting on the recipient's computer, and all of the writer's well-intended graphics disappear.

Example

Hypothetically, the writer wants his readers to know that an emergency meeting has suddenly been scheduled for the day after tomorrow. Observe the following development.

The writer's first draft looks like this:

> The White Winds project is behind schedule due to unforeseen complications in acquiring suitable spares, testing software, and receiving clearance for the initial run. An emergency meeting has been scheduled for 8 a.m. on August 7. All members of the project team should report to the Black Room at that time.

The writer then reads what he's written and decides he had better emphasize his main point, and so he boldfaces the crucial sentence.

> The White Winds project is behind schedule due to unforeseen complications in acquiring suitable spares, testing software, and receiving clearance for the initial run. **An emergency meeting has been scheduled for 8 a.m. on August 7.** All members of the project team should report to the Black Room at that time.

On *his* screen, his main point now stands out very nicely. But will it appear in boldface on the readers' screens? The writer (wisely) is unsure, and so he behaves sensibly—to emphasize the main point, he summarizes it and puts it first.

> All members of the White Winds project team are to report to the Black Room at 8 a.m. on August 7. This emergency meeting has been called to determine precisely what we can do in order to get the project back on schedule. Topics to be discussed include how we can best expedite clearance for the initial run, rapidly finish debugging the software, and more promptly receive necessary spare parts.

This version is much better than the previous ones, but the writer now thinks that the paragraph is a bit long for the reader's comfort. Nothing in particular stands out. And so he isolates the crucial sentence. The result looks like this:

> All members of the White Winds project team are to report to the Black Room at 8 a.m. on August 7.

> This emergency meeting has been called to determine precisely what we can do in order to get the project back on schedule. The issues to be settled are how we can (1) best expedite clearance for the initial run, (2) rapidly finish debugging the software, and (3) more promptly receive necessary spare parts.

This final version is by far the most emphatic. It is the very best any writer can do, given the graphics limitations inherent in most contemporary email applications. (If you are concerned by the old adage that "a paragraph must contain more than one sentence," please rest assured that it does not hold true in business, technical, and scientific writing. Like so many of the phony restrictions that haunt writers (e.g., *Never split an infinitive, Never start a sentence with "because," Never use the passive voice*) it is properly regarded not as a rule, but as hand-me-down folklore.)

4. Keep paragraphs short.

Lengthy paragraphs complicate reading in any medium. Keep them short. Give the page plenty of white space so that it invites reading.

Rather than indenting when beginning a new paragraph, skip a line instead. Doing so will more clearly indicate the separation of topics, increase white space, and make the page more inviting. (See the example on pages 167–168.)

5. Check your spelling and punctuation.

If the document is important, the writer should ensure that it is written well. (If it is unimportant, it should not be written at work.) At a minimum, writing well must mean paying attention to the mechanics of language (spelling, capitalization, number use, punctuation, and so on).

This point should not require much elaboration, but it is amazing how many writers, charging madly ahead under the banner of "It's only email," simply neglect to proofread their work. The same individuals who take pride in their writing when the product is on paper—who revise their memos, letters, and reports—somehow cannot seem to take the electronic medium seriously.

Well, one thing is certain. Sloppy writing reflects a sloppy mind, and that's as true in email as it is anywhere else. If the writer's email application doesn't have a built-in spellchecker (most of the older ones do not), does it follow that spelling doesn't matter? Can the writer not look twice, on his own, to make sure he has had the common courtesy to prevent these distractions to reading?

I think that the same holds true for every other aspect of mechanics. It is simply decent behavior to make things easy on the reader—and "minor" errors in punctuation, grammar, capitalization, and the like not only distract the reader from the writer's thought, but they provoke her to begin proofreading (not to mention the damage they do to the writer's credibility). Worst of all, these errors strongly suggest that the subject of the email is not to be taken seriously.

Here's an example of an all-too-typical email message in the work environment. I didn't make this one up; the writer has given me permission to use it, so long as he remains anonymous.

> My feeling is that the systems described i.e. (MJG, and IPP) are elaborate cuff records designed to capture and manpiulate data at its basic level and provide unit managers with a status of project costs and the capacity to project costs of future/similar projects. I can give you a list of the possible hurdles/barriers to the sucess of these systems if your interested.

For our quick analysis, we do not need to know what a "cuff record" is. We are concerned here not with whether the jargon of "budgetspeak" has been used appropriately, but rather with the writer's casual attitude toward mechanics. There are two misspelled words in this short paragraph. The next-to-last word is incorrectly used. Punctuation runs wild (the device *i.e.* should be inside parentheses, with a comma after it, and no comma should go after *MJG*). The slash, which is used twice, forces the reader to guess at the writer's intention. For example, consider the expression *future/similar*. If the writer had not been in such haste—in other words, if he had taken the occasion seriously—he would have weighed the meanings of these words and recognized that the word he means is *similar*. "Future" goes without saying. If you haven't done a thing yet, you cannot go back and do it in the past; if you do it at all, you will do it "in the future." Many people would argue, with justification, that the first sentence is simply too long to be easily understood. Finally, consider the phrase *project costs*, which occurs twice in that long sentence. The first time we encounter it, it signifies *the costs of a project*. The second time we encounter it (four words later), it signifies *the ability to predict costs*. The same phrase. Opposite meanings.

What's fascinating about this is that the writer knows better. He knows how to spell, he knows that *your* is the wrong word, and he knows how to use *i.e.* He knows how to punctuate, too, and if he were writing a memo or letter he would never have written *hurdles/barriers* or *future/similar*. He knows better. If he were writing in any medium other than email, he would never have written such a long first sentence, and he certainly would have revised the troublesome use of *project costs*. He knows better. But this was only email.

Writers with such a casual attitude about mechanics

should understand that many readers print out email and regard it as they would regard an ordinary memo. A surprising number of readers habitually do this, finding it easier to read the text on paper than on the screen.

6. Send it only to the right people.

The Internet makes it easy to broadcast oneself and one's ideas, but the promiscuous broadcasting of information strikes many people as discourteous (and worse). Target your audience. Resist the temptation to send the email to all of the assistant vice presidents if the true reason you are sending it to them is to prove that you have done some work.

When a writer habitually sends electronic messages to people who do not need these messages, something interesting happens. The reader sees that he has received email. He opens his "In" box. He notices the email name of the writer. He associates the name of this writer with numerous irrelevant messages. (The first five times he received email from this writer, he innocently opened it, read it, and scratched his head, wondering what it had to do with him.) This time, without reading the message, the reader highlights it, opens FILE, and clicks on TRASH. Who can blame him? For this reader, the writer has established a reputation as one who cries *Wolf!* when there is no wolf. After a very short time, people weary of false alarms.

And then, when his readers do not act on the information in his email—do not show up for the meeting, do not respond by the deadline, do not adopt his suggestion—the writer asks them, in frantic bewilderment, "Didn't you read my email?" The honest answer is "no," and the honest reason is that the writer's reputation as a purveyor of irrelevance prevented them.

7. Be courteous.

In its brief existence, email has spawned several words that characterize discourtesy unique to the medium. *Spamming* is used to describe (1) the act of spewing a message indiscriminately to myriad uninterested readers and (2) targeting an individual's mailbox to receive hundreds (or thousands) of junk mail messages. *Flaming* is used to describe the act of ferociously ridiculing, in email (and on a bulletin board for all to see), another person's previously posted ideas.

There will always be hoodlums among us, in cyberspace as well as everywhere else. So long as there are opportunities for mischief, the hoodlums will make the most of them. I think we'd all agree that flaming and spamming are rude. What might not be quite so obvious, though, are the other ways in which writers of email offend their readers

Attempts at humor frequently backfire. The reader of email cannot hear your voice, look at your face, and/or see your gestures and discern that you are joking. Yes, this is true of all writing—but in business writing, humor is certainly not expected, and writers who would never succumb to silliness in a memo often cannot resist it in email. Consider the following passage.

> You've asked whether the problem lies with the hardware or the software. It's the software, Stupid.

The writer doesn't mean to insult the reader by calling her stupid. Instead he intends an allusion to the chuckleheaded slogan from a political campaign, *It's the economy, Stupid*. He thinks that "Stupid" is actually a vaguely affectionate term (that is *his* association with the context). He also believes that the slogan is well known, and so he assumes his reader (1) knows it and (2) will understand his clever reference. The only problem is that the reader doesn't associate the remark in the way the writer intends. Instead, when she reads the sentence, her jaw drops and her face turns bright red. Then, depending on her personality, she bursts into tears, fires off an infuriated response, or fixes the perplexed writer with a killing stare the next time they meet. Adding a "happy face" after the word *Stupid* is one way around this problem. "Happy faces," however, were summarily banished on pages 164–165, and are no longer available. By far the best solution is to resist the temptation to be humorous. At work, simply be straightforward.

In precisely the same way, attempts at irony frequently come across as earnest statements. Consider the following attempt:

> I've just received something called the Simplified Harassment Policy. Has harassment been simplified? I hope so. I never understood how to harass people before. Now maybe I will.

The writer has his tongue planted firmly in his cheek, but he forgets that his reader cannot see his bulging cheek or the merry look in his eyes. Why would any writer run the risk of a humorless reader assuming that *Now maybe I will* is an earnest statement? Readers are people, and people are offended for all sorts of reasons, many of which the writer cannot possibly predict or control. Communication is tricky enough in the best of circumstances. When you write in the workplace, resist the twin temptations of humor and irony.

One additional note regarding inadvertent insults. A lot of people believe, for some reason, that email TEXT IN ALL CAPS suggests the writer is shouting. This may be tantamount to my insisting that all dogs are horrible because a dog once accidentally nipped me when I was a child. (Such thinking is called hasty generalization, and it may be the most common of logical fallacies.) Be that as it may, whether these readers are right or wrong is beside the point; if they have such a knee-jerk reaction to ALL CAPS, the savvy writer must respect it. However, so far as I know, readers of email do not object to ALL CAPS used as headings.

8. Keep it brief.

In business, practically by definition, email messages should be relatively brief. Issues that require a lengthy treatment are customarily printed out and circulated as formal reports and memos. This is because everyone tacitly acknowledges that reading from a piece of paper is easier, more comfortable, than reading from the monitor.

One of the best uses of an email message is to "cover"—succinctly introduce—a longer document that you send via the "Attach File" function in your software. Typically, the longer document is one that you have spent some time writing and revising. In such cases, all your message has to do is alert the reader (1) that you are including another document and (2) indicate why you are sending it, or why it is important (if the reader doesn't already know).

Some Warnings About Electronic Mail

At many organizations (maybe even at most organizations), management has the ability to intercept and monitor employees' email. Whether this is ethical or not is a debate for another time; it happens, and that's the point here. I doubt you would find a written policy regarding email monitoring anywhere, but it happens routinely, and not only in intelligence organizations but in the business and regulatory environments as well. The moral, of course, is that you should think twice before you forward that long, spicy joke to your friend in the Seattle office. You should think twice before you send a coworker an email that suggests unusual complications in an executive's ancestry. In business it's usually best to remain business-like.

Another important thing to understand about email is that it can be deleted "until the cows come home," but it will survive somewhere in the ghostly limbo of electronic ether. Let me tell a short anecdote.

Recently, at a large organization headquartered in Washington, D.C., an employee was let go. He was terminated for reasons the organization termed "his consistently subpar performance." He sued the organization, claiming he had been the victim of malicious gossip carried over email. The organization's lawyers scurried to "suggest" that employees delete every last message containing any reference to the plaintiff. They believed they had succeeded in erasing all the evidence.

What they had successfully done was *delete* all of the email. There is a world of difference between deleting and obliterating. The former employee's attorney hired technical experts and, armed with a court order, succeeded in resurrecting the deleted messages. Many of the messages could aptly be characterized as malicious assassination of character, and they bolstered the former employee's contention that his performance had suffered because of a hostile environment.

The organization had little choice but to settle before trial.

Once again, let's set ethical questions aside. The practical point is that what you write in email may as well be engraved in stone. An old Roman proverb says it best: *Once sent, the voice can never be recalled.* If you remember this adage, and remember also that your reader deserves your best effort, you will take care with your writing in electronic mail.

Part Five
CD-ROM Functionality

CD-ROM Functionality

The *Write for Results* CD-ROM has been designed to ensure that users can access information quickly and easily. You will find all the topics in the menus at the beginning of each section. Click on the topic of your choice and you are on your way. You will always know which section you are working in by checking the heading at the top of the screen.

Another useful feature is the hypertext links between different sections. These have been color-coded and will take you to a section offering additional information. Click on the return button to jump back to your original starting point.

Double-clicking on the "click here" and "show me" buttons on some screens will reveal pop-up windows containing additional information, an intersting anecdote, or the answers to questions.

The *Write for Results* CD-ROM also enables you to test your knowledge in three different ways. At the end of each topic in the Learn to Write for Results section, you will find a Practice Your New Skills exercise.

Type-in areas throughout *The Writer's Toolkit* will enable you to try your hand at answering some of the questions. You will find the answers in the Show Me boxes, which you can access by clicking on the icon.

The Evaluate Your Writing Skills sections contains a test containing twenty-five questions. At the end of the test you will be given a list of all the topics you need to review.

In the Create Your Own Document section you will be able to use a library of existing letters, taken from *The AMA Handbook of Business Letters,* and adapt them for your own use.

This section includes tools for searching, retrieving, and editing the letters of your choice. There are three ways of searching for a particular letter in the database that contains 324 ready-to-use letters. You can use the keyword search or select specific criteria, or you can scroll through the entire list in The Letters Library.

Keyword Search

Open the Keyword Search Dialog box (Figure 1) by clicking on the Keyword Search item in the Create Your Own Document menu. Scroll through the list of available keywords and choose a keyword or several keywords that best describe the letter you are looking for (Figure 2).

Select Specific Criteria

Open the Criteria Selection Dialog box (Figure 3) by clicking on the Select Specific Criteria item in the Create Your Own Document menu.

This dialog box (Figure 3) begins with three sets of search criteria: Business Transactions, Business Relationships, and Employment. Begin by selecting one of these criteria. Advance to the next set of criteria by clicking the "next" button. This makes it easy to compile search criteria on a screen-by-screen basis (Figure 4).

When you reach the end of your search, the Criteria Search Results Dialog box (Figure 5) will appear and list the letters that match the criteria you selected. From this screen you can preview the letters, edit them, or save them to My Favorite Letters, creating a list of the letters you think you will find most useful.

My Favorite Letters

You can compile a list of your favorite letters from any of the Search Result Dialog boxes (Figure 6) found in the Create

Your Own Document section of the *Write for Results* CD-ROM.

You can save as many letters as you need in your "favorites list" and then access them at any time, using the File menu or by clicking on My Favorite Letters on the Create Your Own Documents menu (Figure 7).

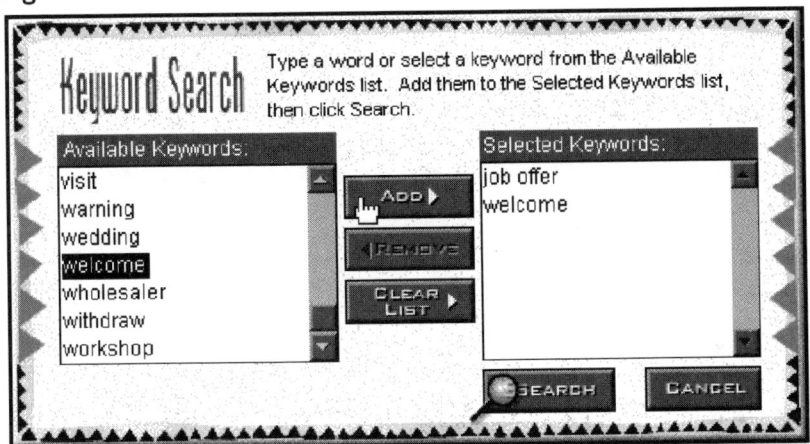

Figure 1

Keyword Search — Type a word or select a keyword from the Available Keywords list. Add them to the Selected Keywords list, then click Search.

Available Keywords:
- visit
- warning
- wedding
- **welcome**
- wholesaler
- withdraw
- workshop

Selected Keywords:
- job offer
- welcome

[ADD] [REMOVE] [CLEAR LIST] [SEARCH] [CANCEL]

Figure 2

Keyword Search Results   Click on a document in the 'documents found' window to view its contents below.

12 Documents found

- Job offer, including conditions of employment
- Job offer, including bonus structure
- Job offer, including stock options
- Accepting job offer
- Rejecting job offer
- Letter to applicant who has accepted job offer
- **Welcoming new employee**

Welcoming new employee

Dear Mr. *[last name]*:

We look forward to your arrival here in *[location]* and having you as part of the *[company name]*. We were pleased when you accepted our offer of employment, and are sure that you will be a valuable employee.

↑ SAVE TO FAVORITES LIST   ↑ EDIT THIS DOCUMENT   CLOSE

CD-ROM Functionality

Figure 3

> **Select the criteria that best describes your business letter:**
>
> ○ **Business Transactions**
> Letters in this section cover a wide range of activities associated with conducting business on a daily basis. These include requests, responses, offers, corrections and follow up letters.
>
> ○ **Business Relationships**
> In this section the letters cover many social aspects of conducting business such as invitations, thank you, congratulations and giving information about people and promotions.
>
> ⦿ **Employment**
> These letters cover a range of activities associated with employment issues, including job applications, job offers, recommendations, change in status and terminations.
>
> next   CANCEL

Figure 4

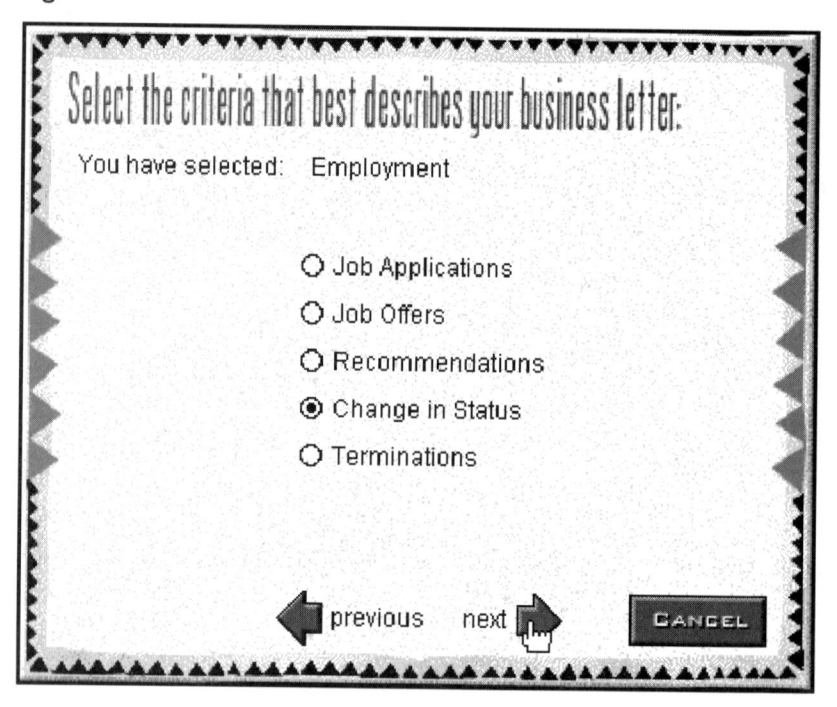

Figure 5

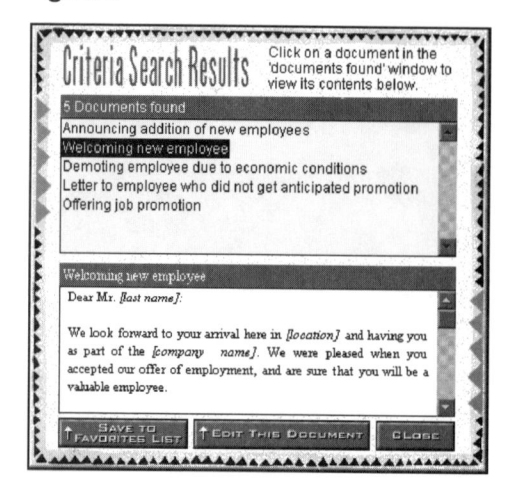

CD-ROM Functionality

Figure 6

List of Letters

Click on a document in the 'documents found' window to view its contents below.

Business Letters A - Z

Abbreviated version of project status letter
Accept part payment and confirm new payment schedule
Accepting informal invitation
Accepting invitation to contribute an article to a publication
Accepting invitation to speak at an event
Accepting invitation to speak at workshops
Accepting job offer

Accepting informal invitation

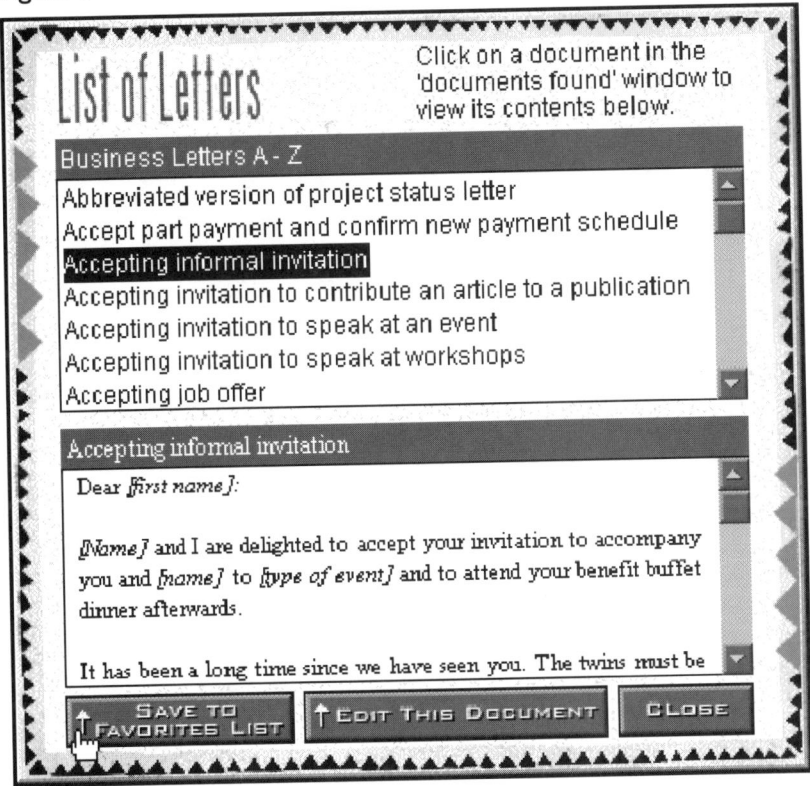

Dear [first name]:

[Name] and I are delighted to accept your invitation to accompany you and [name] to [type of event] and to attend your benefit buffet dinner afterwards.

It has been a long time since we have seen you. The twins must be

SAVE TO FAVORITES LIST   EDIT THIS DOCUMENT   CLOSE

Figure 7

File
Print screen text
Select Word Processor
Open Favorites List
Exit

My Favorite Letters
click here

Index

: (colon), 120–123
   with quotation marks, 143
... (ellipsis points), 132
[ ] (brackets), 119–120
— (dash), 130–131
   with quotation marks, 144

a, an, 96–97
abbreviations, 96, 137
acronyms, 96, 137
active voice, 35–38
adjectives
   comma between, 123–124
   compound, 72–73, 134–135
adverbs, avoiding unnecessary, 34–35
affect, 91
ambiguity
   avoiding, 14–16, 133
   definition of, 112
ambiguous, 87
and/or, 149–150
apostrophe, 115–119
   in contractions, 115–116
   in plurals, 119
   with possessives, 116–119
archaic words, avoiding, 94–95
assumptions about writing, 13

be advised that, 97–98
biannual, 102
bimonthly, 17–18
biweekly, 102

brackets ([ ]), 119–120
brevity, 38
   conciseness vs., 29
   in electronic mail, 171, 177
   and sentence length, 60
   and tone, 42
business writing, 9–12

CD-ROM (included with book), 183–188
The Chicago Manual of Style, 7
choosing words, *see* word choice
clarity of meaning
   and conciseness, 29–30
   and modifiers, 61–62
   and punctuation, 106–109, 112
   and redundancy, 45–46
   and style, 14
   and word order, 54–57
clause(s)
   definition of, 112–113
   dependent, 112–113, 155–156
   independent, 121–122, 125–126, 146–147, 151–158
   relationships between, 150–158
clichés, 93–94, 100–101
coining words, 99
colon (:), 120–123
   with quotation marks, 143
comma, 123–130
   after *i.e.* and *e.g.*, 127–128
   with contrasting elements, 124–125

comma (*continued*)
  with direct quotations, 129
  before *etc.*, 128
  with independent clauses, 125–126
  before *Jr.*, 129–130
  in list of items, 125
  with modifying phrases, 126
  with nonessential words/phrases, 124
  in numbers, 129
  in parallel constructions, 129
  with quotation marks, 143, 145–146
  as separator, 123
  with time expressions, 126–127
  with titles, 128–129
comparing ideas, 76
complexity, avoiding needless, 19–20
compound adjectives, 72–73, 134–135
compound nouns, 134
conciseness, 15, 29–53
  and active vs. passive voice, 35–38
  and avoiding redundancy, 42–52
  and avoiding *to be*, 32–34
  and avoiding unnecessary adverbs, 34–35
  and avoiding unnecessary repetition, 52–53
  brevity vs., 29
  and clarity of expression, 29–30
  requirements of, 30–31
  and use of verbs, 31–32
  and word choice, 38–42
connotations, 97
contractions, apostrophe in, 115–116
contrasting elements, 124–125

conveying ideas, 16–17
"cramming in" ideas, 78–79
cross-references, 138

dash (—), 130–131
  with quotation marks, 144
dependent clause(s), 112–113
  followed by independent clause, 155–156
  independent clause followed by, 156
difficult words, redundant explanations of, 46

economy of expression, 10
e.g., 96–97, 127–128, 138
either . . . or, 69–70
electronic mail, 161–179
  brevity in, 171, 177
  courtesy in, 175–177
  emphasis in, 169–171
  getting to the point in, 166–169
  at home, 162–163
  paragraph length in, 171
  potential of, 161–162
  and privacy, 177–179
  sending, 174
  spelling and punctuation in, 171–174
  Subject line in, 165–166
  in the workplace, 163–165
The Elements of Style, 12
ellipsis points (. . .), 132
emphasis, 54–80
  dash for, 130–131
  in electronic mail, 169–171
  with hyphenation, 70–75, 135
  illogical, 46–49
  and modifier placement, 60–70
  and parallel structure, 75–80

Index

and subject-verb-object order, 57–60
essential language, nonessential vs., 114
etc., 128
euphemisms, 93–94
even, as modifier, 68
exaggeration, avoiding, 101
exclamation point, with quotation marks, 144–145

flaming, 175
foreign words and phrases, 95
for your information, 98
Franklin, Ben, on choosing words, 82, 83
"funhouse" structures, 58

gerunds, 119
Get Ahead Toolkit series, 1
good faith, in writing, 31
grammatical dogmatism, avoiding, 80–81

herein, 94
herewith, 94
however, 157
hyphen, 70–75, 133–137
  and emphasis, 70–72, 135
  function of, 72–73
  use of, 73–75

ideas
  comparing, 76
  conveying, 16–17
  "cramming in," 78–79
  listing, 76–78
  and sentence length, 59–60
  unclear, 85
  visualizing, 88
i.e., 96–97, 127–128, 138

illogical emphasis, 46–49
impact, 91
impatience of readers, 20–22
implement, 100
Inc., 129–130
independent clause(s), 112, 113, 151–158
  colon with, 121–122, 146–147
  comma with, 125–126
  dependent clause followed by, 155–156
  followed by dependent clause, 156
  list of three or more, 156
  with longer conjunction, 154–155
  with short conjunction, 153–154
  without conjunction, 151–153
institute, 100
institutions, apostrophe with, 118
irony, 141, 176
-ize words, 93

jargon, 95–96, 100
Jr., 129
just, as modifier, 69

Latinate words, 18–19
"legal-sounding" terms, 94
lists (series), 113–114
  colon with, 121
  comma in, 125
  of ideas, 76–78
  parentheses in numerical, 137
  punctuation in, 109–110, 111, 113–114
  semicolon in, 147–148
Ltd., 129–130

may, 92
memos, 92

modifier(s), 60–70
  at beginning of sentence, 62–63, 126
  and clarity of expression, 61–62
  either . . . or/neither . . . nor as, 69–70
  at end of sentence, 63–64
  even as, 68
  just as, 69
  and meaning, 60–61
  in middle of sentence, 65–66
  only as, 67–68
  that as, 67
  which as, 66

naming, 99–100
neither . . . nor, 69–70
nonessential language, essential vs., 114
not un- constructions, 49–52
nouns
  compound, 134
  possessive forms of, 116–119
  selecting, 89
  writing with verbs instead of, 31–32, 99
numbers
  comma in, 129
  hyphen with, 133
  parentheses in series of, 137

obviously, 98
omitted words
  comma for, 129
  ellipsis points for, 132
only, as modifier, 67–68
organizations, apostrophe with, 118

parallel structure, 75–80
parentheses, 137–139

parenthetical expressions, 114–115
  dash with, 130–131
passive voice, 35–38
period, 139–140
  with parentheses, 138–139
  with quotation marks, 142–143
phrases, 115
place names
  apostrophe with, 118
  comma with, 128
plurals, apostrophe with, 117, 119
possessives, apostrophe in, 116–119
potentially, 93
precision in writing, 88–89
prefixes, hyphen with, 133
proofreading, and punctuation, 111–112
punctuation, 105–158
  and clarity of meaning, 106–109, 112
  with clauses, 112–113, 150–158
  in electronic mail, 171–174
  limitations of, 106–107
  as necessity, 109–110
  with parenthetical expressions, 114–115
  and proofreading, 111–112
  purpose of, 105
  and reading speed, 107–108
  in series, 111, 113–114
  see also individual punctuation marks

question mark, 140–141
  with quotation marks, 144
quotation marks, 141–142
  colon with, 143
  comma with, 143, 145–146
  dash with, 144
  exclamation point with, 144–145

Index

period with, 142–143
question mark with, 144
semicolon with, 143–144
single, 142
with titles, 142
quotations
  brackets with, 119–120
  commas with, 129
  ellipsis points in, 132

ratios, 122
reader
  "boiling down" by, 15
  effort by, 13–14
  impatience of, 20–22
  misunderstandings by, 15–16
reading, 87–88
redundancy, 42–52
  as illogical emphasis, 46–49
  as intended clarification, 45–46
  with *not un-* constructions, 49–52
  testing for, 43–45
repetition, avoiding unnecessary, 52–53

semicolon, 146–148
  with quotation marks, 143–144
sentence(s)
  in electronic mail, 169–171
  ideas and length of, 59–60
  modifier at beginning of, 62–63, 126
  modifier at end of, 63–64
  modifier in middle of, 65–66
  parallel structure in, 75–76
series, *see* lists
shall, 91–92
single quotation marks, 142
slash, 148–150
speech, writing vs., 22–24

spelling
  in electronic mail, 171–174
  and style, 8
standard English, 10, 22
style, 7–26
  and ambiguity, 14–16
  and avoiding dogmatism, 80–81
  and avoiding of needless complexity, 19–20
  and clarity of meaning, 14
  and conveying ideas, 16–17
  defining, 7, 9
  and effort by writer, 13–14
  and impatience of reader, 20–22
  precepts of, 9–12
  scope of, 7–9
  simplicity in, 15, 18–19
  in speech vs. writing, 22–24
  and spelling, 8
  and variety, 24–26
  and word meanings, 17–18
  with word processing software, 8
style guides, 7
style sheets, 7
subject(s)
  with one verb, 150–151
  with two verbs, 150
subject-verb-object order, and emphasis, 57–60
support, 92–93
suspended compounds, 134
symbols, 137

technical terms, 141
testing, for redundancy, 43–45
that clauses, 67, 92
these, 92
those, 92
time expressions
  comma with, 126–127
  hyphen with, 133–134

titles
  comma with, 128–129
  quotation marks with, 142
to be, avoiding, 32–34
tone, and brevity, 42

unit modifiers, 72–73
unnecessary repetition, avoiding, 52–53

variety of style, 24–26
verb(s)
  and active vs. passive voice, 35–38
  and avoiding *to be,* 32–34
  one subject with two, 150
  two subjects with one, 150–151
  writing with, instead of nouns, 31–32, 99
visualizing, 88
vocabulary, 85–86

which clauses, 66
word choice, 82–102
  and acronyms/abbreviations, 96
  and archaic words, 94–95
  and changing meanings, 101–102
  and clichés, 93–94, 100–101
  common problems in, 91–102
  and conciseness, 38–42
  confidence in, 89–91
  and connotations, 97
  and euphemisms, 93–94
  and exaggeration, 101
  and foreign words, 95
  and jargon, 95–96, 100
  and knowing meanings of words, 86–87
  and length of words, 82–83
  in memos, 92
  precision in, 88–89
  and reading, 87–88
  tips for, 85–91
  and using nouns as verbs, 99
  and visualizing, 88
word length, 82–83
word meanings, and conciseness, 30, 47–48
word order, 54–70
  and clarity of expression, 54–57
  and hyphenation, 73
  and modifier placement, 60–70
  subject-verb, 57–60
word processing software, and style, 8
words
  meanings of, 17–18
  thinking with, 39–40
writing process, 13–14